ANNE OF CLEVES

For F.C. Troughton

ANNE
of
CLEVES
Fourth Wife of Henry VIII

Mary Saaler

THE RUBICON PRESS

The Rubicon Press
57 Cornwall Gardens
London SW7 4BE

First published 1995
Reprinted 1997

British Library Cataloguing-in-Publication Data

A catalogue record for this book is available from the British Library

ISBN 0-948695-41-2

Printed and bound in Great Britain by Biddles Limited of Guildford
and King's Lynn

Contents

Illustrations

Cover. Anne of Cleves. Holbein's portrait of her was pleasing to Henry VIII. (*Louvre, Paris.*)

Anne of Cleves. The portrait has been attributed to the workshop of Barthel Bruyn (1493-1555). It was sold in London in 1930 and its present location is unknown. (*Christie, Manson and Woods Ltd.*)

Thomas Cromwell was created Earl of Essex in 1540. He was the King's chief minister 1533-40. (*National Portrait Gallery, London.*)

Anne of Cleves. This portrait has also been attributed to the workshop of Barthel Bruyn. X-ray photography has revealed the inscription 'Anne, by grace of God Queen of England, daughter of John, third Duke (of Cleves)' above her right shoulder. (*By kind permission of the President and Fellows of St John's College, Oxford.*)

Henry VIII painted by an unknown artist c. 1542. (*National Portrait Gallery, London.*)

Mary Tudor at the age of 28, painted by Master John. (*National Portrait Gallery, London.*)

Bletchingley, Surrey. The gatehouse is a visible remnant of the former large Tudor country-house. (*Graham Brooks.*)

Hever Castle, Kent. Anne received Hever Castle in 1540 as part of the divorce settlement .(*By kind permission of Hever Castle Ltd.*)

Penshurst Place, Kent. Anne gave up Bletchingley and received Penshurst Place in exchange. (*By kind permission of Lord De L'Isle.*)

Acknowledgements

This book arose as a result of archaeological excavations at Bletchingley, in Surrey. These have revealed the foundations of the house where Anne of Cleves lived after her divorce from Henry VIII. When I began to investigate the history of the house, I became intrigued with Anne's life and how she dealt with being an ex-queen.

Anne of Cleves has been written as an expression of thanks to the residents at Bletchingley who, over the years, have shown great forbearance and kindness to the archaeologists digging trenches through their gardens. I am also grateful to members of the Bourne Society for all their hard work and good humour. Thanks are also due to the Surrey Archaeological Society for help in obtaining documents and to Graham Brooks for photography. Furthermore, I wish to acknowledge permissions kindly granted to me by Gael and Toby Falk, the British Library, the Folger Shakespeare Library and the Department of Manuscripts, University of Nottingham. Crown Copyright material is reproduced with the permission of the Controller of HMSO.

Finally, I should like to thank the staff and postgraduate students at University College London for their help and encouragement, which have enabled me to produce this book.

Mary Saaler

The area of the Lower Rhine in the early sixteenth century. (Fig. 1)

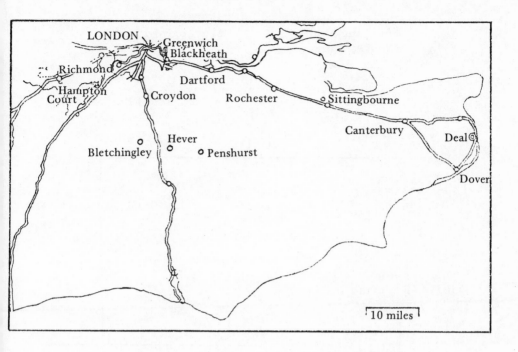

Places in south-east England associated with Anne of Cleves. (Fig.2)

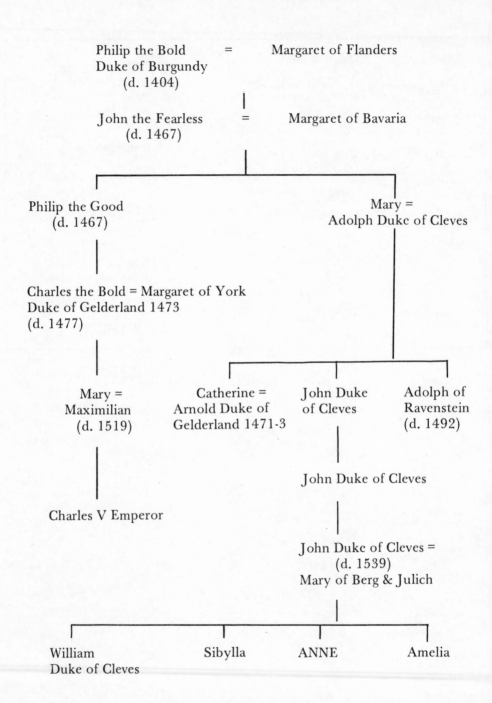

Philip the Bold   =   Margaret of Flanders
Duke of Burgundy
(d. 1404)

John the Fearless   =   Margaret of Bavaria
(d. 1467)

Philip the Good   Mary =
(d. 1467)   Adolph Duke of Cleves

Charles the Bold = Margaret of York
Duke of Gelderland 1473
(d. 1477)

Mary =   Catherine =   John Duke   Adolph of
Maximilian   Arnold Duke of   of Cleves   Ravenstein
(d. 1519)   Gelderland 1471-3   (d. 1492)

Charles V Emperor   John Duke of Cleves

                                      John Duke of Cleves =
                                              (d. 1539)
                                      Mary of Berg & Julich

William   Sibylla   ANNE   Amelia
Duke of Cleves

Connections between the Houses of Burgundy and Cleves. (Fig. 3)

Introduction

Anne of Cleves, Henry VIII's fourth Queen, has generally suffered from what we might describe as a 'bad press'. This book is an attempt to redress the balance.

Since she was Queen for only six months and a little-known foreigner, she has failed to attract the kind of attention that has been focused on the personalities, careers and families of Henry's other wives. However, after her divorce from Henry, she stayed in England, where she lived as a member of the royal family and was accepted into royal circles. She did not disappear into obscurity.

On the whole, comments about her by historians have been largely unflattering, based on Henry's reaction to her. It is difficult for us, at such a distance in time, to judge her qualities and it is perhaps even more difficult to decide what any man would consider appealing in a woman. But it is clear that, whatever she looked like, Henry did not find her attractive. Although he did not make the comment that he was presented with 'a great Flanders mare', the words sum up his feelings about Anne of Cleves.

Male historians have no problem in accepting this reaction. Hume, who was writing in the early 1900s, took a totally censorious and chauvinistic view of Anne, describing her as 'blessed with a happy insensibility of temper, large, bony and masculine, the very opposite of the type of beauty which would be likely to stimulate a gross, unwholesome voluptuary of nearly fifty'. He also referred to the 'coarse boorishness of the petty German court' from which she came, implying that she was a woman of so little refinement that she took great pleasure in the luxury and recreation that she found in England.[1]

Later historians have presented less extreme views. Nevertheless, Pollard referred to the 'serio-comic episode of Anne of Cleves' and Scarisbrick described her as 'disappointing', having a flat personality that led her to accept a life of obscurity, with resignation. He suggested that, while her portraits presented a fairly agreeable appearance, her personality was at fault—she was dull, shy, lacking both charm and fire. But he did mention that she was clever enough to keep her head, which was more than Thomas Cromwell and her successor, Catherine Howard, achieved.[2] Scarisbrick's view of her dull personality is echoed in later writers:

> It is difficult, when looking at Anne's portrait, to see why Henry took such great exception to her as her face is distinctly pleasant. One can only conclude that she was a dull, unaccomplished young woman without conversation or wit and the very opposite of what Henry sought and found most attractive in women.[3]

On the other hand, while Starkey referred to the marriage as 'the whole Anne of Cleves fiasco', he did concede that Anne's handsome settlement allowed her to live in comfort and has suggested that we should recognize her 'skilful reaction to what might have been a personal disaster'.[4]

Women historians have generally tended to take a more sympathetic view of Anne, paying more attention to her personality than to her looks. Strickland, writing about Anne in the 1850s in the *Lives of the Queens of England*, presented her as a victim of circumstances and used words like 'the ill-treated, much-injured Princess, the luckless bride', regarding her as a woman who possessed gentle virtues, in contrast to Henry, who was 'her coarse-minded consort, with a countenance stamped with all the traces of the sensual and cruel passions which deformed his mind'. Strickland emphasized Anne's character—her good sense and amiable temper, her queenly dignity and her placid, domestic virtues. She also laid some of the blame on Anne's unfashionable and outlandish clothes that caused her to appear ugly, saying that she had the most magnificent wardrobe of any of Henry's wives, but the worst sense of dress.[5]

Later women writers have also looked upon Anne with a certain charity, stressing that her ability to survive a difficult and potentially dangerous situation shows that she was perhaps the wisest of Henry's wives—she was certainly the luckiest. They have also emphasized her adaptability to English ways, which allowed her to live in peace and contentment as a 'country gentlewoman'. Her acceptance of her situation has led Fraser to remark, 'Her behaviour during her bewilderingly short marriage and the many confusing years in a foreign land which followed, displayed a touching dignity; she deserves sympathy not derision'.[6] But, while such qualities might be admirable in a woman, they were certainly not exciting enough to arouse Henry's interest.

Apart from divergent views about Anne's personality and appearance, there have also been different views regarding her religion. Her marriage to Henry was welcomed by Protestants at the time and, on the whole, historians have assumed that because she came from Germany, she must have been a Protestant. Strickland even went so far as to describe her as 'our Lutheran Queen'. This opinion seems to have persisted, with later references to her as 'a Protestant bride'.[7] However, before she died, Anne took confession and she asked to be buried as a Catholic. This has been explained as evidence that she changed her religion in later life, possibly to suit the King. In fact, like Henry, she was a Catholic and remained a Catholic throughout her life. Cleves itself, although it had links with Protestant countries, remained a Catholic country.

Apart from the legal complications, divorce has always been emotionally difficult, particularly since there is a tendency to impute blame or guilt to one or other of the parties. Who was to blame for the failure of the Cleves marriage? Anne and Henry were so unsuited to one another that the blame would seem to lie squarely with Thomas Cromwell, who attempted to use the marriage to advance his political ambitions. In the event, Anne prospered because Henry's views on divorce were coloured by his previous experience with Catherine of Aragon, who kept him waiting for nine interminable years. As a result, the King's desire for a speedy divorce enabled Anne to gain a favourable settlement and live her life as she chose, in reasonable comfort. This leaves us with Starkey's conclusion, that she may have been more expert in money matters than in sex.[8]

I The Search for a New Wife

The search for a new wife for Henry VIII lasted nearly two years. After the death of Jane Seymour in 1537 the King's notorious treatment of his previous wives made women unwilling to face the risks of an uncertain future as his next Queen. The King's health was also causing concern. Early in 1537, John Husee wrote to Lord Lisle, the governor of Calais, 'The King seldom goes abroad because his leg is so sore'; a few months later, Henry himself wrote to the Duke of Norfolk, 'to be frank with you, which you must keep to yourself, a humour has fallen into our legs, and our physician advises us not to go far in the heat of the year'. Hans Holbein's painting of the King in 1541 commemorating the royal grant of a charter to the company of barber surgeons shows his swollen and bandaged leg discreetly masked by his richly brocaded cloak. In such a situation, the King hardly appeared as an attractive husband to any prospective bride. Ludovico Falier, the Venetian ambassador at Henry's court sent back to the senate of the Republic of Venice the following description of Henry. He saw him as a tall man—'his face angelic rather than handsome, his head imperial (*Caesarina*) and bald and he wears a beard, contrary to English custom.' There is no other evidence for the King's baldness; all his portraits depict him wearing a hat. The ambassador also referred to Henry's growing irritability and meanness, which had replaced a former affable, generous and gracious manner. After many refusals and failed negotiations, the idea of a marriage between Henry and Anne of Cleves seemed a brilliant solution to an awkward problem. The architect of the marriage, Thomas Cromwell, was the King's chief minister and Lord Privy Seal—a man of immense practical ability and energy, with a deep concern for the good of his country.[1] If his plan had succeeded, he would have secured a perfect union of matrimonial, religious and political forms. Unfortunately, it failed on all three points, bringing disappointment to Anne and Henry and disaster to Cromwell.

Because of his need for a male heir and a secure succession, Henry had already found ways to end his first two marriages, which had produced only daughters, the two Princesses Mary and Elizabeth. He knew he was capable of producing a male child. While he was still married to his first wife, Catherine of Aragon, he had many love affairs. One of his mistresses, Elizabeth Blount, who was related to William Blount, Lord Mountjoy, chamberlain to the Queen, had produced a son in 1519. This boy was named Henry Fitzroy; the use of this surname, meaning 'the King's son', was a clear indication of the boy's status. Fitzroy later received the title of Duke of Richmond, and his education and upbringing were suitable for the son of a Prince. The dukedom of Richmond echoed the title of Edmund Tudor, the King's grandfather, who became Earl of Richmond in 1453. The award of such a title may have been an indication that, although he was illegitimate, he might be considered as a potential heir, if Henry had no other sons.

With two daughters and an illegitimate son, the succession was always a matter of great concern. Henry had made use of Cromwell's considerable political skills to shake off the authority of the Pope and make himself supreme head of the Church in England. This had allowed him to obtain a divorce from Catherine of Aragon, mother of Princess Mary, in spite of the combined opposition of the Pope and the Emperor Charles V, Catherine's uncle. An important factor in the King's marital instability was the presence at court of a large number of attractive young women. Like Elizabeth Blount, they were related to the courtiers and some were maids of honour to the reigning Queen. Their office gave them access, not just to the Queen, but to influential officials within the royal household. It is no coincidence that three of the King's wives, Anne Boleyn, Jane Seymour and Catherine Howard had been maids of honour to the previous Queen. Backed by their powerful and ambitious families, they used their office to attract the King's attention and provide him with amusement and entertainment when he was bored. While he was still married to Catherine of Aragon, Henry became entranced by the charms and wit of Anne Boleyn, whose younger sister, Mary, was already his mistress. Eventually, in 1533, Anne became his second wife and the future mother of Princess Elizabeth. But, after Anne's pregnancies failed to produce a male heir and Henry's interest in her charms had faded, she was executed on unproved charges of adultery. In reality, the evidence against her amounted to no more than gossip, scandal and hearsay, willingly provided by the ladies of her court. Even while Anne was still alive, his roving eye had lighted upon Jane Seymour who then became his third wife. But Jane had died in 1537, hardly two weeks after providing him with a long-desired male heir. The official announcement recorded the birth:

> By the provision of God, Our Lady St Mary, and the glorious martyr St George, on the 12th day of October, the feast of St Wilfred, the vigil of St Edward, which was on the Friday, about two o'clock in the morning was born at Hampton Court Edward, son to King Henry VIII.

Great excitement at the birth of the new heir shows in the letters that were sent out from the Queen's office at Hampton Court on October 12th 1537. They emphasized the King's joy and pleasure at the birth of a Prince and referred to the prospect of 'quiet and tranquillity for the kingdom', which would result from a secure succession.[2] As soon as the birth was announced, fires of joy were lit in the streets; there were banquets and cheers and shooting of guns day and night. Messengers were sent out to all the cities in the kingdom and were rewarded with great gifts as they spread the good news. Henry had at last achieved his life's ambition of securing the prospect of a peaceful transition from his reign to the next.

A few days later, the baby Prince was baptized with great ceremony and rejoicing in the chapel royal at Hampton Court. As soon as he was christened, all the torches in the chapel were lit, and all his titles were proclaimed, including those of Duke of Cornwall and Earl of Chester. The Princesses Mary and Elizabeth were present; Mary, who was then 21 years old, stood as godmother to the new prince. His godfathers were the Dukes of Norfolk and Suffolk and Thomas Cranmer, Archbishop of Canterbury. After the christening, the baby was presented to the King and Queen and received the blessing of God, the Blessed Virgin Mary and St George.[3] Such an arduous christening ceremony may have affected the Queen's health. Certainly, she did not fully recover from the effects of childbirth and, in spite of the attentions of William Butts, Henry's personal physician, she died just a week after the christening. She was buried in St George's Chapel, Windsor, where Henry was buried beside her ten years later. He had a hatred of sombre mourning clothes but he showed genuine sadness and affection for her by wearing mourning clothes for three months after her death. Edward Hall, in his chronicle of the reign of Henry VIII, described Jane's funeral and the impact of her death on the King. It stands in stark contrast to his delight at the birth of the new Prince.

> Lord, what lamentation shortly after was made for the death of his noble and gracious mother Queen Jane, and of none in the realm was it more heavily taken than of the King's majesty himself, whose death caused the King immediately to remove unto Westminster, where he mourned and kept himself close and secret a great while. The King's majesty kept his Christmas at Greenwich in his mourning apparel, and so was all the Court till the morrow after Candlemas day, and then he and all other changed.[4]

The infant Prince had his own household and, because of Henry's great concern for his heir, he was mostly kept away from London, to avoid risks to his health. He lived first at Havering in Essex until, in 1539, his household moved to Hunsdon House in Hertfordshire. This was a house that the King had taken over and greatly enlarged, making it into a 'palace royal'. Princess Mary was living there in 1536. It lies at about 20 miles to the north of London and was within a convenient distance for Henry to visit his son whenever he wished.

Henry's marriage with Jane Seymour had lasted less than two years. While his second wife, Anne Boleyn, was pregnant once more, Henry had been attracted to Jane, daughter of Sir John Seymour and a maid of honour to Anne. Already, Jane's two brothers, Edward and Thomas, were notable and handsome members of Henry's court. Edward had done particularly well by becoming a gentleman of Henry's Privy Chamber. Following the birth of the new Prince, Jane's eldest brother, Edward, was created Earl of Hertford, while Thomas, the younger brother, was knighted. Edward Seymour was high in the King's favour and was closely linked with Sir Nicholas Carew, Henry's master of horse. Carew was heavily involved in the promotion of Jane Seymour and coached her in the right ways to attract the King. Jane's attraction for Henry seems to have lain in her quiet and submissive demeanour, which was in complete contrast to his two previous wives—to the fiery and passionate temperament of Anne Boleyn and the stubborn character of Catherine of Aragon. Even while Anne was awaiting execution at the Tower on the morning of Friday, May 19th 1536, Jane was waiting for the news at Carew's house at Beddington, in Surrey. On the same day as the guns at the Tower announced the death of Queen Anne, Jane's betrothal to Henry became public. At the end of May, they were married. Unlike Anne Boleyn, Jane was never crowned. Her coronation, which was set for the end of October, was postponed twice and then never took place. The contrast between the two wives led Sir John Russell to comment 'the King hath come out of hell into heaven, for the gentleness in this and the cursedness and unhappiness of the other'.[5] Jane's quiet dignity and gentle attempts at reconciliation within the royal family caused Henry to remark (in retrospect) that he had loved her best of all his wives.

After Jane's death, there had been many marriage plans for Henry, as Cromwell began his search for a new wife for the King. Political changes on the continent and the desire for a new wife caused the King to look for an alliance abroad with a foreign royal family. Above all, a royal lady from a foreign country was less likely to be the tool of ambitious, competitive, English noble families seeking to promote their own interests at court. The court was a place of struggles for power, it was unstable and no one knew who to trust. In the words of John Husee, every man was there for himself. The King himself was the source of patronage and power, while the court around him was made up of rivals for his favours.[6] Pretty young women of these noble families played a key part in attracting the King's favour and patronage, to the benefit of their relations. In this situation, a foreign marriage would diminish the influence of the English nobles and establish Cromwell's position at the heart of the court. However, because Henry's reputation had spread far and wide, amenable foreign brides were not easy to find. There were rumours in royal courts abroad that he had poisoned Catherine of Aragon; everyone knew that he had executed Anne Boleyn, and there was gossip that Jane Seymour had died in childbirth because of neglect.

Henry was looking for closer links with France. His relationship with Francis I, the King of France, veered continually from friendship to enmity. The tremendous gathering at the Field of Cloth of Gold in 1520 had meant to symbolize the friendship between the two monarchs and the two countries. Sir Richard Wingfield, the English ambassador in Paris, stated that the aim of the meeting was for the Kings to make 'such an impression of entire love' that shall 'never be dissolved, to the pleasure of God, their both comforts and the weal of Christendom'.[7] Cardinal Wolsey, Henry's chancellor and chief minister, had organized the meeting on behalf of both Kings. It involved taking more than 5000 people from England and supporting them for a month in France in the style of a royal household. Dress, display and appearance were important to Henry; when he was not engaged in sport 'he glittered like a peacock'.[8] The Field of Cloth of Gold was a perfect opportunity for him to show the splendour of his court. Richard Gibson, master of hales (temporary buildings), tents and pavilions, excelled himself by setting up a magnificent canvas banqueting-house, painted to look like brickwork and decorated inside with cloth of gold and silver. Wolsey had organized a brilliant setting for his master, a 'view of earthly glory—today the French all clinquant, all in gold, like heathen gods, shone down the English, and tomorrow, they made Britain (shine like) India'. (*Henry VIII* act 1 scene 1).[9] While the pageantry and symbolism were magnificent, the gathering resulted in heavy financial costs to both countries; the personal encounters between Henry and Francis brought no political benefits, it added up to no more than a show or entertainment.

Despite the splendour of the occasion, there was no permanent friendship between the two countries. Even while Henry was in France, the Emperor Charles V was in England, being royally entertained at Dover and Canterbury on a visit that lasted for five days. When Charles returned to Calais, Henry met him there for secret talks where the two men were united in their opposition to Francis. As a result of their planning, an English army arrived in France in 1523, led by the Duke of Suffolk. Although the army marched through France and was in sight of Paris, the Duke brought his men back to Calais, without making any important territorial gains. In 1525 battles between Charles and Francis resulted in the capture of Francis and, taking advantage of the French King's difficulties, Henry contemplated a further invasion, with the prospect of taking Paris and being crowned King of France. However, Henry changed his mind—no invasion took place. Instead, through Wolsey, he negotiated with the Regent of France, mother of Francis, to help her son gain his freedom. As a result of this arrangement, Francis and Henry were no longer in opposition; they drew up a new treaty of friendship and this time they were united against Charles V.

Against such a shifting background of alliances and opposition, with further realignments taking place in the 1530s, Henry was looking for closer links with France in 1538, after the death of Jane Seymour. Jane's death provided him with an opportunity for a link through marriage. As a consequence, Cromwell began making enquiries about likely French royal ladies as Henry's future wife. Most of our information about Henry's quest for a wife comes from the letters written by foreign ambassadors to their rulers—the Spanish ambassadors in France reported to their Emperor, Charles V, while the French and Spanish ambassadors in England also sent their reports of events back to France and Spain. These men acted as spies and relied on picking up bits and pieces of court gossip and rumour, true or untrue. Because they were looking for political advancement, they were always keen to report items that were favourable to themselves and their masters and play down the significance of bad news. For this reason, their information was likely to be biased. However, in surveying the reports of several ambassadors, we can arrive at some kind of common story.

Cornelius Scepper, the Spanish ambassador at the French court, sent reports on some of the opening moves in Henry's search for a wife. Sir Francis Bryan was in France on Henry's behalf. Bryan was Henry's close and trusted friend. His father had been at court during the early years of Henry's reign and the two young men remained good friends. Bryan shared the King's taste in amusements and literature and he had taken an important role at the christening of Prince Edward. He was a man whom Henry trusted with the delicate business of setting marriage plans in action. Bryan took the initiative by suggesting that Henry should come to Calais, which was then an English garrison town. Bryan planned that, while remaining on English soil, Henry should meet Margaret, Princess of Navarre, who would bring with her seven or eight young women of royal blood, of the families of Lorraine, Nevers and Vendôme. At such a meeting, Henry would be able to view the ladies and so make his choice. Margaret of Navarre was chosen to lead the delegation as she was the sister of the French King, Francis I, and it is thought that her daughter Jeanne may have been one of the young women to be considered.

At first Francis helpfully offered his full co-operation in promoting a marriage alliance with England. There were certainly plenty of royal French ladies to choose from, but he was reported to be annoyed at Henry's request to see a selection of prospective brides before making his choice. Francis disliked the fanciful idea of French ladies of noble birth being trotted out to be viewed by their future husband, like horses being put on show at a fair. He sarcastically suggested that Henry might even like to try them out beforehand to find which one suited him best. Francis also took the view that if one of them was chosen to be Queen, the other women, however beautiful they were, would suffer at being rejected. He wisely refused to allow his own daughter to be put in competition with the rest, sensing the trouble that would arise, if she was among those rejected. The Queen of France took a similar view; she refused to take any part in such a show and declared that she was not 'a keeper of harlots'. One of the ladies included in the 'shopping list' was of the family of Vendôme who was then a nun in a convent, which led the High Constable of France to remark,

I have no doubt that, as the King of England considers himself a Pope in his own kingdom, he would have preferred the nun to any other daughter of the royal blood in France.

The ambassadors reported Henry's anger and disappointment at the storm of protest at his request. He was upset since he had anticipated full co-operation from the French King.[10]

In spite of the protests, Francis was still happy for Henry to marry a French Princess if the procedures were carried out in a more conventional way. He suggested to his ambassador, Gaspard de Coligny, Lord of Castillon, that any other noble French lady, except his royal cousin, Marie of Guise, might be a suitable bride for Henry. Marie was ruled out because she was already promised in marriage to James V, King of Scotland. But this prohibition against marrying Marie had the effect of firing Henry's interest and determination to have her for a bride at all costs.

In December 1537 Castillon was still writing to Francis about the prospects of a French marriage for Henry. He wrote that the King had heard such great praise of Marie that he was now more determined than ever to have her as his next wife. Her widowhood did not deter him and he was heard to declare that since he was 'big in person, he had need of a big wife'. Henry refused to consider other French brides; he turned down marriage with Francis' daughter, Margaret, because at fifteen he felt she was too young to be his wife, and he dismissed Marie of Vendôme, another royal cousin, who had also been considered as a prospective bride for James V, on the grounds that she was 'the King of Scots' leavings'. He had become obsessed with the idea of marriage with the prohibited Marie of Guise and, according to Castillon, he could not keep off the subject. There were even rumours that Henry would have given 'half his kingdom' for her. Marie, however, had different ideas, and soon set out for Scotland, where she married James V.[11]

When the prospects of a French marriage alliance faded, Cromwell put forward the idea of a match with Christine, the beautiful daughter of Christian, King of Denmark. Denmark was then a Protestant country and the prospect of a marriage link with Denmark fitted with Cromwell's plan to build up a religious and political union of non-Catholic states on the continent to counter-balance the Catholic powers of Francis I and Charles V. But Christine, then aged about 16, who had previously been married to the Duke of Milan and was already a widow, cautiously rejected Henry's offer. Holbein had already painted the portrait of the beautiful young woman as a prospective bride for Henry; the painting now hangs in the National Portrait Gallery in London and shows the pale delicate skin of her face emphasized by her dark mourning clothes of rich furs and velvets.

There was strong opposition to this marriage on the continent, where people were suspicious of an alliance that would place the two kingdoms of Denmark and Norway under the control of the King of England. Coincidentally, there was a similar concern about the growing influence of Cleves, as the Duke of Cleves was trying to expand his territorial possessions.[12] There had even been discussions of a marriage link between Christine and the Duke of Cleves, but these too came to nothing.

After such a series of fruitless marriage negotiations across the continent, Cromwell finally suggested Anne of Cleves as a prospective bride, probably assuming that she resembled her beautiful elder sister Sibylla and so would appeal to Henry.

At the beginning of 1539 Anne of Cleves was 23 years old and about half Henry's age. Admittedly, it was unusual for a Princess, even of a small duchy, to be unmarried at 23; in contrast, her elder sister, Sibylla, was married at the age of 14. Anne was born on September 20th 1515, one of the four children of John, Duke of Cleves, and his wife Maria. John was also ruler of the adjoining provinces of Mark and Ravenstein, while Maria was the heiress to the lands of Julich and Berg, which then became united with Cleves. Their children were William, who succeeded his father as Duke of Cleves, and three girls, Sibylla, Anne and Amelia. Their eldest daughter, Sibylla, had married John Frederick, Duke of Saxony, who was the leader of a federation of Protestant states in Germany, known as the Schmalkalden League. Sibylla, who was famous both for her beauty and her personality, was considered to be one of the most outstanding women of the time. Their second daughter, Anne, first entered the public scene at the age of 11, when political considerations led to negotiations for a marriage with Francis, the eldest son of the Duke of Lorraine. A marriage treaty was drawn up in 1527 between the two young people, but this formal marriage arrangement was never followed up and Anne remained at home with her mother and her younger sister, Amelia. Anne learned to read and write and could read the Bible in German and, even though she did not study classical languages, she absorbed current intellectual and religious ideas.[13]

II   Religious and Political Background

Cleves was a small part of the kingdom of Germany which, in turn, was part of the much larger Holy Roman Empire. Germany itself was divided into principalities, duchies, kingdoms, which were sometimes united in alliances, but often at war with one another. Marriage alliances were a critical factor in political advancement and Cleves had been closely allied to the House of Burgundy through a series of dynastic marriages. During the fifteenth century, the Burgundian court was the most brilliant in western Europe, excelling even the courts of England and France in splendour. As part of the expansion of Burgundian power, the sister of Philip the Good, Duke of Burgundy, had married Adolph, Duke of Cleves in the mid-fifteenth century. Philip used his Cleves connections and went on to organize the marriages of his Cleves nieces and nephews to suit his own needs, with the ultimate ambition of establishing a kingdom of Burgundy in the area of the lower Rhine. In particular, his niece, Catherine of Cleves, was married to Arnold, Duke of Gelderland; another niece, Margaret of Cleves, was married first to the Duke of Bavaria and then to the Count of Wurtemburg. He made his nephews, John, Duke of Cleves, and Adolph of Ravenstein, members of the prestigious Order of the Golden Fleece and, in effect, Cleves became a client state of Burgundy.[1]

The duchy of Cleves itself had also acquired extra territories by marriage. For example, the counties of Mark and Cleves were united in 1368; then the Duke of Berg became Count of Julich in 1423 and, in 1511, by the marriage of John, Duke of Cleves, to Mary of Berg and Mark, the four small duchies were united under one ruler. Like many other German states, Cleves maintained its own army and its own ducal court.

While at first glance, Cleves might seem to be the home of an insignificant provincial court, it gained importance and prestige because of its links with the Dukes of Burgundy and the splendour of the Burgundian court. The marriage of Charles the Bold, son of Philip the Good, to Margaret of York, sister of Edward IV, at Bruges in 1468 was a superb example of Burgundian extravagance. It reached new heights of display and splendour, with shows of magnificent pageants, tableaux and jousting, becoming one of the most splendid and extravagant celebrations in the whole history of Burgundy. John Paston went to Bruges in Princess Margaret's retinue and wrote a description of the ducal court to his mother, Margaret:

> As for the Duke's court, as of lords, ladies and gentlewomen, nights, esquires, and gentlemen, I have never known like to it, save King Arthur's court.

Of the Burgundians taking part in the jousts he said:

> of such gear, and gold and pearls and stones, they of the Duke's court lack nothing, by my troth, I heard never of so great plenty as here is. [2]

The Burgundians showed their splendour through their possessions—their costume, jewellery, retinues and buildings. The purpose of such lavish display was to emphasize the greatness and importance of the ruler. Although the court of Cleves was less splendid and less wealthy, the close connections between the Houses of Cleves and Burgundy, added status and lustre to the ducal court at Cleves.

However, marriage alliances also brought threats and conflict. The Dukes of Burgundy had made serious inroads into German lands during the fifteenth century and Cleves itself was drawn into a long-lasting dispute by Charles the Bold's intervention in Gelderland, which lay to the north of Cleves. The acquisition of Gelderland formed part of Charles' grand plan to extend Burgundian power. His aim was to build a sufficient power-base to allow him to become Holy Roman Emperor in succession to Frederick III. Internal disputes and civil war gave Charles an excuse to intervene in Gelderland and he took over the duchy in 1473, imprisoning the rightful ruler, Adolph, Duke of Gelderland. Charles installed his own administrative system and ruled it harshly:

like an iron-fisted conqueror, intent on the outright incorpora-
tion of new territory into the political and administrative
framework of his own lands.

In November 1473, there was a magnificent celebration at
Trier in Germany to mark Charles' take-over of Gelderland. At
the celebration, Charles met the Holy Roman Emperor, Frederick
III, and did homage and fealty to him for Gelderland. Like the
wedding of Charles the Bold, the event was marked by ostenta-
tious display. The Duke's clothes were overwhelmingly splendid,
being cloth of gold and decorated with pearls, diamonds and
rubies. One of Charles' leading supporters at the meeting was
John, Duke of Cleves, also brilliantly dressed in cloth of gold. It
was a magnificent occasion of great feasting, jousting and entertainment.[3] At the conference, Charles hoped to be rewarded with
the succession to the imperial throne; he gained recognition of his
conquest of Gelderland and other small states, but the final
triumph eluded him. Ironically, it fell to his grandson, Charles V,
to succeed to the imperial throne in 1519. This came about by a
dynastic marriage; after Charles the Bold died in 1477, his daughter and heiress, Mary of Burgundy, married Maximilian, who
succeeded Frederick III as Emperor. As a result of this marriage
alliance, the Burgundian lands passed into the control of the
empire, not to any of the German states.[4]

In the sixteenth century, the power of the Burgundians had
already waned. The changing political situation on the continent
had resulted in an alliance between the French King, Francis I, and
Charles V of Spain, grandson of Charles the Bold. In 1519 Charles
V had succeeded to the imperial throne, following the death of his
father, Maximilian. As Holy Roman Emperor, he controlled a vast
empire covering the present-day countries of Austria, Hungary,
Germany, Holland and Belgium, Spain and some parts of Italy.
Within the German part of the empire lay various German states
which belonged to the League of Schmalkald, headed by John,
Duke of Saxony. The league was formed in 1531 in opposition to
the proposed coronation of Ferdinand, the brother of Charles V
and Archduke of Austria, as the King of the Romans and successor
to Charles V. While the rest of the Holy Roman Empire supported

the Pope and the Catholic church, these German states sympathized with Martin Luther in his protests against the Roman Catholic church and in his challenge to the authority of the Pope. Luther's ideas were taken up rapidly in Germany, where there was already a strong tradition of dissent. From this platform, his influence soon spread beyond Germany and his writings aroused international interest. Reports from across Europe show how people were keenly interested both in his writings and his personality. His views were attractive not only to radical dissenting reformers but also to those who were looking for reforms from within the Catholic church—'no corner of Europe was entirely safe from the resonance of the German controversies'.[5]

Lutheranism threatened the doctrines of Catholicism by teaching people that they could achieve salvation without depending on the sacraments of the church. In 1538 the spread of such ideas caused Pope Paul III to propose a Catholic alliance between Francis I and Charles V, offering the prospect of a Catholic crusade against England after Henry had rejected the authority of the Pope. The threat of such a Catholic invasion and Henry's reluctance to accept the extreme ideas of Lutheranism ultimately led Cromwell to propose a marriage alliance with Cleves. While Cleves was not itself a Protestant state, Cromwell aimed to use its connections with Protestant states in Europe to provide England with a counterbalance to the powers of the Pope, Charles V and Francis I.

Henry set out his own views on Catholic orthodoxy when he published the Statute of Six Articles in 1539, otherwise known as 'a whip with six strings'. Open opposition to Cromwell's administrative reforms had already begun to surface in 1536, arising especially from the dissolution of the smaller monasteries, which was a prelude to greater changes in the administration of the church. The first protests occurred at Louth in Lincolnshire, where the rising was crushed without much difficulty. Soon a larger rebellion spread across the northern counties of England in a formidable symptom of discontent. It came to be called the 'Pilgrimage of Grace'. This was followed by other outbreaks of rebellion, confronting Henry with the severest crisis of his reign. The rebellions were savagely put down, but they had the effect of showing Henry the power of traditional religion in the country and the bitter resentment towards change and reform. Having crushed the rebels, he then published his Statute of Six Articles which reaffirmed the essential beliefs of the Catholic church and set fierce punishments, including death by burning, for those who dissented. The King was attempting to present traditional Catholic ideas within his own national framework, emphasizing that his quarrel was with the Pope, not with the Catholic church. As supreme head of the church, he wanted to regulate religion in England in a way which conformed with his own views. However, in spite of protests and rebellion, the dissolution of the monasteries continued, while shrines and images were destroyed.

Although the House of Cleves was connected with the Protestants through marriage and politics, the Dukes of Cleves, like Henry VIII, looked for reform in the Catholic church but did not accept the extreme views of Lutheranism. In addition, there was a further link between England and Cleves which pre-dated these marriage negotiations. This link came through the teachings of the great Dutch scholar, Erasmus. The ideas of Erasmus centred upon making the scriptures, meaning the New Testament, accessible to all who wished to read them. In this way, all people, whether laymen or clergy, could look back to the teachings of Christ and find enlightenment and simple truths. The publication of the Bible in English was part of the process to make enlightenment available to the general population and to give people access to the 'word of God'. These ideas of humanism were distinct from the Lutheran movement; they aimed to sweep away Catholic conservatism while challenging the extreme views of the Protestants. It was an exciting time for religion and learning, as these principles of humanism led people to believe that a golden age was about to emerge through the rebirth of true Christianity.

Some humanists looked upon Luther as an ally in reform, but Erasmus clearly saw the dangers of Lutheranism because of the backlash of conservative reaction it aroused against reform. Even before the reformation, an interest in classical scholarship at the universities of Oxford and Cambridge had already stirred an interest in the humanist movement and so the ideas of Erasmus fell on fertile ground in England. Humanism gently promoted the 'middle way' of moderation, offering education and knowledge as practical remedies for the problems of society. This humanistic approach later became incorporated into the 'middle way' of the English church.[6] While Erasmus was spreading such humanist ideas in England, one of his associates, Conrad Heresbach, was councillor to the Duke of Cleves and became tutor to his eldest son, William, when he reached the age of seven. With the aid of Heresbach and Erasmus, John, Duke of Cleves promoted moderate reform in the Catholic church in Cleves through the publication of the Church Ordinance in 1533. This produced a peculiar church order, which the Duke ruled as its spiritual head—it was reformed, but it was not Protestant. Although his eldest daughter was married to the leader of the Protestant states, the Duke himself rejected outright Protestant ideas and banned the writings of Luther because they were 'vain, wrong and heretical'.[7]

In 1538, William, son of the Duke of Cleves, had assumed the title Duke of Gelderland and thus incurred the anger of Charles V, who claimed the duchy by right of his imperial inheritance. However, the previous ruler, Charles of Gelderland, who had ruled it for the empire on behalf of Charles V, took the surprising step of abandoning his allegiance to the Emperor shortly before he died in 1538 and bequeathed his country to Francis I. In the event, the people of Gelderland wanted neither of these as their ruler and chose William of Cleves as Duke of Gelderland. With the addition of Gelderland, which gave it access to the sea via the Zuyder Zee, Cleves now developed a strategic importance in the area of the lower Rhine; a situation which was unwelcome to both France and Spain. William had cleverly succeeded in establishing Cleves as a powerful state in north-west Germany. By having control of the territory on both sides of the Rhine, he was able to control the route which linked Charles' territories in Italy and southern Germany with his lands in the Netherlands. Although William's possessions were small, they presented a threat out of all proportion to their size.

By June 1538 France and Spain were again united in their hostility to England—the friendship between them was so close that Charles V was allowed to travel across France to crush a revolt in Ghent—this unity led Cromwell to intensify his enquiries about a matrimonial alliance with Cleves. The friendship between France and Spain also threatened William of Cleves and an alliance with England had considerable appeal for him. William followed the teachings of Erasmus and the religion of his duchy remained a reforming compromise between Rome and Lutheranism. In its form, it was broadly similar to Henry's church. In this situation, with one sister who was already married to the Duke of Saxony, William was ready to accept an alliance with England. Two marriages were suggested: one between William, son of the Duke of Cleves, and Princess Mary, and the other between Anne and Henry VIII.

Against this background, in January 1539 Cromwell's proposal of a matrimonial alliance between England and Cleves seemed a logical outcome, based on religious and political motives. The religious climate was similar in both countries, where the rulers supported reform, but were not Protestants. Politically, an alliance would form a link between England and the League of Schmalkald, providing a useful counter weight to the Catholic alliance of Charles V, Francis I and the Pope.

Three leading men were at the heart of the negotiations dedicated to bringing about the marriage alliance between Cleves and England, as a way of forging links between England and the Protestant states on the continent. These were Thomas Cromwell, who was Henry's chief minister, Henry Olisleger, chancellor of Cleves, and Francis Burchart, vice-chancellor of the Duke of Saxony.

However, the prime mover in all the negotiations was Cromwell. In effect, he staked his career and finally his life on the success of the marriage. In contrast to most of the men around him, he had come from humble origins. He had no powerful family to support him. He was born around 1485; the son of a man who held just a few acres of land in Surrey and had tried a variety of lowly occupations. Cromwell left home as a young man and went abroad to advance his career. He served as a soldier and went on to work in businesses in Italy and the Netherlands. He used his travels to acquire a knowledge of foreign languages. During these years he also visited the large mercantile centres of Bruges and Antwerp, where he built up useful contacts with the English merchants. This is the period when he was reckoned to have learned by heart Erasmus's translation of the New Testament—an indication of his religious leanings. When he returned to England in 1513, he married well and turned his attention to law, business and money-lending. He served as a Justice of the Peace in Surrey and he took up a position in Wolsey's administration in 1514. Wolsey, the King's chief minister, was quick to recognize his extensive skills. Probably with Wolsey's help, Cromwell first became a Member of Parliament in 1523 and, by 1525, he was acting as the cardinal's chief agent in the dissolution of the smaller monasteries.

He was a man dedicated to work and he immersed himself totally in the details of administration. Others recognized his abilities:

through a singular excellence of wit, joined with an industrious diligence of mind, and help of knowledge, he grew to such a sufficient ripeness of understanding and skill—that he was thought apt and fit for any room or office where he should be admitted.

Cromwell's 'witty demeanour' clearly attracted the King's favour and he first entered royal service in 1530, when he became one of the King's advisers. After Wolsey's downfall later that same year, Cromwell set himself up as the King's expert in dealing with Parliament, where he had considerable influence—'Mr Cromwell penned certain matters in the Parliament house, which no man gainsaid'. The King was quick to make full use of his considerable administrative skills. He soon became Henry's principal adviser and, by 1531, Cromwell was a Privy Councillor. His rise was meteoric. In 1533 he was Chancellor of the Exchequer and the following year he was Secretary of State. His abilities enabled him to carry through the reformation acts of 1532-9 that resulted in the Act of Supremacy and made Henry head of the English church. As vicar-general for 1535 and as Lord Privy Seal and the King's deputy, he organized the dissolution of the remaining monasteries in 1536-9. In 1539 he became Lord Great Chamberlain and, the following year, his career culminated with the award of the earldom of Essex.[1] These great offices were given to him as rewards for his abilities and were not necessarily powerful in themselves. In addition, Cromwell was not particularly interested in just a show of power; he lived in a fairly modest style and was content with simple surroundings. The real significance of his offices lay in his relationship to the King—they were a sign that he enjoyed Henry's full confidence in his administrative reforms. He was unquestionably single-minded in his pursuit of power, with the object of establishing the absolute authority of the monarch in his realm. Unfortunately, his great skills aroused the jealousy of English courtiers who felt that their traditional role was usurped by a self-made 'new man'. But perhaps continental diplomats and politicians were less aware of the 'newness' of Cromwell and failed to take into account the resentment and envy that he aroused in England.

Certainly, Cromwell applied himself keenly to the task of cementing the Cleves alliance. Letters and commands passed frequently between England and Cleves throughout 1539. Cromwell conducted his negotiations through agents; of these, Christopher Mount, the English envoy in Cleves, played a crucial part in the proceedings. Henry also used Mount as an intermediary and wrote to him in January 1539 asking him to make detailed enquiries about the religious opinions of John, Duke of Cleves, and his son William. Henry wished to find out for certain whether they were 'still of the old popish fashion' or whether they were inclined to change their views. At the same time, Cromwell wrote to Mount instructing him to remind Burchart about earlier discussions between them of a marriage between William of Cleves and Princess Mary. He also asked Mount to make enquiries about the beauty and qualities of Anne of Cleves, to assess 'her shape, stature and complexion' and find out if she was likely to appeal to the King. Cromwell, taking a practical view, judged that a portrait would settle the matter and ordered Mount to obtain one. In typical Cromwellian style, he played his hand cautiously and told Mount not to demand it openly but to suggest tactfully that the House of Cleves might send a portrait of Anne for Henry's consideration. In January, Cromwell was still in favour of a 'cross-marriage', with Princess Mary marrying William and Henry marrying Anne, but the idea of such a double alliance faded in time.[2]

There was a lull in the negotiations on the death of John, Duke of Cleves, in February 1539. His son, William, then succeeded him as Prince of Julich, Gelderland, Cleves and Berg, Duke of Mark, Zutphen and Ravensberg, and Lord of Ravenstein—an expanse of territory which gave him a considerable power-base in the area of the lower Rhine. But Charles V was seeking to take over Gelderland, which he claimed as heir to his grandfather, Charles the Bold. In this situation, William looked for allies and he turned both to England and to John, Duke of Saxony, leader of the Protestant states in Germany. The states were united in their opposition to Charles V, but William, like Henry VIII, remained a reforming Catholic and did not formally join the League of Schmalkald.

Against this complex background of events, Christopher Mount had to ensure that, for the sake of appearances and in an attempt to preserve the King's dignity, the Duke would offer his sister to Henry in marriage; it was not right for the King of England to appear as a suitor, searching for a bride. It was truly a crucial time for Cleves, when 'circumstances had conspired to confer a considerable diplomatic and strategic lustre upon Cleves'.[3]

Cromwell's office soon became busy with the arrangements. In March 1539 the King's envoys at Cleves, Edward Carne, Nicholas Wootton and Richard Berde, were ordered to approach Duke William to find out if he was still in favour of the match between Anne and Henry and to 'have a sight of his eldest sister'. At the same time Cromwell, cautiously wrote to Mount reminding him to use trustworthy messengers on the King's business or, if none were to be found, to send his letters by sea via the port of Hamburg, where Dr Robert Barnes, a Lutheran and an associate of Cromwell, had made suitable arrangements for the dispatch of letters.[4] As well as being an agent for Cromwell, Barnes also served as Henry's envoy to Denmark, Scandinavia and Cleves.

A distinct obstacle to the negotiations was the earlier marriage contract between Anne and Francis of Lorraine which had never been formally renounced. Olisleger, chancellor of Cleves, being keen to promote an alliance with England, gave his opinion that the contract was no longer in force and that Anne was free to marry anyone she might choose. However, the vagueness of this decision had drastic repercussions for Anne at a later date. Because of the lingering doubts about the pre-contract, Anne's younger sister, Amelia, was also included in the negotiations—just in case she needed to be considered as an alternative bride for Henry.

William of Cleves was in a difficult position; he wanted the support of England over his claim to Gelderland but, before committing one of his sisters to such a marriage, he needed to be sure about the future Queen's status in England. The English envoys took a different view of his hesitation and suspected him of using delaying tactics to gain as much as possible from the alliance. But Olisleger on the other hand, seeing the advantages of such a match, which would bring 'great honour, strength and advancement to the House of Cleves', hurried matters along and promised to provide portraits of both Anne and Amelia 'within 14 days', saying, that they had been ready for months.[5]

Mount sent back reports to Cromwell about both Anne and Amelia. He clearly preferred Anne to her sister, saying that everyone admired her appearance and her character. He emphasized her good qualities, her honesty, her modesty and her serenity 'one said that she excels the duchess as far as the golden sun excels the silver moon'.[6] (We cannot tell from Mount's statement whether he was comparing her with her beautiful sister, Sibylla, Duchess of Saxony, or the equally beautiful Christine, Duchess of Milan). Nevertheless, Henry wanted to see for himself what his prospective bride looked like and he ordered Holbein to paint portraits of both Anne and her sister Amelia. Mount vainly tried to advance the process by urging Duke William to employ his own court painter, Lucas Cranach, but the Duke explained that his painter was ill and wisely left the task for Holbein.

Clearly, both Mount and Wootton found it difficult to give a true account of the two sisters because it was impossible for them to get a good, clear view of the women. Wootton wrote that he had hardly caught sight of them and complained about their 'monstrous habit and apparel', referring to their large nun-like head coverings, which prevented him from seeing their faces. Instead of seeing the women for himself, he had to rely on enquiries that he made among the gentlemen of the court and on Olisleger's assurance that the portraits were a good likeness.[7]

Wootton's report to Henry in August sounded a more cautious note than Mount's earlier opinion. He wrote that both Anne and Amelia had been strictly brought up by their mother. From his various enquiries he had discovered that Anne was 'of a very lowly and gentle' disposition; that she and her widowed mother were very close and that she spent much of her time with her needlework. He reported that she could read and write in German, but knew no other languages and had no knowledge of music, since it was not considered a suitable pastime for noble German ladies. However, Wootton hinted at her intelligence and thought that she would soon learn English, when she put her mind to it.[8]

On September 1st, Charles de Marillac, the French ambassador at Henry's court, wrote to the King of France, telling him that Henry had now seen Anne's portrait and that serious marriage negotiations were taking place. He wrote:

> King Henry had sent a painter, who is very excellent in his art, to Germany, to take a portrait to the life of the sister of the Duke of Cleves; today it arrived, and shortly after a courier (came) with secret news for the King, but the Duke's ambassadors are come to treat with the King about the lady.[9]

We do not know for certain which of Anne's portraits Henry saw; it was probably the portrait by Holbein which now hangs in the Louvre in Paris and, finding it pleasing, he went ahead with the marriage plans. A contract was signed in Dusseldorf on September 4th 1539 and later that month the Duke of Cleves sent his own envoys to England, led by Olisleger and Burchart. The object of their visit was to settle the size of the dowry, to negotiate an income for Anne in England, to arrange a widow's pension for her and to secure her future if the King and her brother William died.

Like many of the German rulers, William was short of money and her dowry was an additional obstacle for him. In the event, he agreed to give her 100,000 florins; the same as her elder sister had received. The payment was divided into two amounts: 40,000 florins to be paid on the wedding day and the other 60,000 to be paid in London within a year. The amount was agreed, but there is no evidence to show that it was ever paid and Henry seems to have waived his right to it. In case she should become a widow, her dower rights were settled at 15,000 florins a year and she was to keep all her gold and silver plate. There was also provision for her to return to Cleves, if she wished. A further contract was signed at Windsor Castle on September 24th and the final agreement was made in London on October 4th. The envoys discussed all kinds of practical details, including the arrangements for Anne's journey. William agreed to pay for her travel as far as Calais in appropriate splendour, with gold and jewels and all things suitable, 'as befits such a Princess, the daughter of such noble parents and the intended bride of so great a King'.[10]

The portrait was the keystone in the negotiations—it convinced Henry that the marriage would be successful. There are at least five known portraits of her. Holbein painted the one that is in the Louvre; there is a miniature of her in the Victoria and Albert Museum in London; another portrait hangs in St John's College, Oxford. X-ray examination of this painting has revealed the words *Anna D.G. Regina Angliae Filia Johnnis 3 Duc*–Anne, by grace of God, Queen of England, daughter of John, third Duke (of Cleves). The use of the words 'Queen of England' on this painting point to a time just after the marriage agreement had been signed. A fourth painting, which is very similar to the one at St John's College, has since disappeared. A fifth portrait was sold at auction in London in 1930 and that too has disappeared. The sitter in these three latter paintings wears the same dress–the chief difference lies in the head-dress. The St John's portrait and its similar version have a rather nun-like head-covering, while the fifth painting shows the sitter wearing a flat, circular bonnet. There is just a slight possibility that the similar portraits may show the two sisters, Anne and Amelia but, on balance, the great similarities suggest that they all depict Anne. Three of these paintings were probably the work of Barthel Bruyn or his workshop; he was not the official painter to the court of Cleves, but he sometimes worked for the court.[11]

All of these paintings show a rather expressionless oval face, with a long nose, brown eyes and a pale complexion. In particular, the portrait in the Louvre shows a modest face with downcast eyes, overshadowed by a nun-like veil which was held in place by a jewelled cap, with a gold tassel at one side. In contrast to her face, her clothes dominate the picture–her magnificent dress of red velvet was decorated with bands of gold, embroidered with pearls and rich with jewels–an example of truly Burgundian splendour. There was no further mention of Amelia's portrait–she stayed at home in Cleves with her mother and never married.

With Henry's acceptance of her portrait, Anne's world changed. As Princess of Cleves, Anne's heraldic device was two white swans, emblems of candour and innocence. These were based on a legend associated with the Rhine, the river that runs through Cleves. According to legend, 'the knight of the swan' came to an heiress of Cleves in a boat, guided by two white swans. From the story, the House of Cleves incorporated the swans into its heraldry. The family motto was *Candida nostra fides*–our faith is spotless. But now, instead of being a Princess at a small ducal court, Anne was about to become the future Queen of England.[12]

IV From Cleves to Calais

Until the marriage agreement was finalized, Anne's role was largely passive. But as soon as the marriage arrangements were approved, she became actively involved. Either Anne, or her mother, quickly chose suitable companions who would travel with her to England, and attendants for her court when she arrived there. The seamstresses, needleworkers and embroiderers of Cleves must have been extraordinarily busy, producing elaborate dresses and other clothes not just for Anne, but for all the ladies and gentlemen who travelled with her. In spite of William's pleas of poverty, her clothes and jewellery were magnificent, echoing the Burgundian tradition of display and splendour among the ruling class.

Henry VIII clearly anticipated difficulties for Anne on a journey that involved passing through the Netherlands, which were then part of the empire of Charles V, and through France— areas which were both potentially hostile to England. In a letter among the Spanish State Papers, the Pope's envoy requested both Charles V and Francis I to refuse to grant passage to the Princess of Cleves, 'if it is true she is a Lutheran'.[1] Because of such threats, Henry ordered his map-makers to produce a map showing a safe route for Anne. The chart which they produced is the earliest example of its kind known in England. The availability of money that resulted from the dissolution of the monasteries and the threats of foreign invasion had focused attention on the skills of map-making and brought them into prominence. Maps were seen to be in the interests of government and useful to the security of the kingdom. Henry had realized the advantages of having good maps as a way of discovering weaknesses in the defences of the country and the first English large-scale maps date from the later years of his reign. Since there were no maps or charts showing a route across the sea from Gelderland to England, Henry sent two ship-masters in secret to work out a safe route for Anne's journey. They produced a rutter, or rough chart, of the Zuyder Zee, which was then used as the basis for a map. It was not drawn to scale but it had the practical advantage of showing the areas with the most navigational problems. There may also have been a complementary map showing the approach to London along the Thames estuary. Henry hoped that by travelling first through Gelderland, which her brother controlled, Anne could then sail secretly across the Zuyder Zee and board an English ship for the remainder of the journey across the channel. The map shows how the King planned to have her smuggled across the Zuyder Zee as far as the channel, where she would board the royal flagship.[2] Perhaps because of the difficulties of such a long sea journey in winter, the idea was abandoned and Henry eventually obtained a guarantee of safe-conduct for Anne from the Queen of Hungary, who was the regent of Charles V in the Netherlands. The negotiators from Cleves were pleased when an overland route to the channel coast was chosen, with just a short sea crossing from Calais to England—they had been worried about the effects of a long sea journey on the complexion of the bride, who was so 'young and beautiful'.[3]

Preparations to welcome the new Queen were already under way. On November 5th 1539 Marillac wrote to the King of France that Henry had informed his lords that he expected his bride to arrive 'in about twenty days', and that he was intending to go to Canterbury to meet her.[4] Following the guarantee of safe-conduct, a reception for Anne was planned in Calais, where she would be greeted by the Earl of Southampton, who was Lord High Admiral of England, and various other notables. As early as October 18th, Cromwell had written to Arthur Lisle, the governor of Calais, urging him to inspect the King's house there, called the 'Exchequer', and quickly arrange for any necessary repairs to be made. Lisle was also told to check the streets and lanes and ensure that they were properly paved. None of these orders mentioned Anne of Cleves, but Lisle had been in England a few months earlier, when negotiations for the marriage were being talked about, so he was probably well aware of the reasons for Cromwell's interest in Calais. Lisle himself was not officially responsible for receiving Anne, that was the task of the Lord Admiral, who had overall responsibility for her. Lisle's principal duty was the security of the garrison town.

The Lisle Letters reveal the problems of organizing the visit. Correspondence flowed between John Husee in London, who was Lisle's chief contact and representative in England, and Lisle in Calais; the main objective was to discover the date of Anne's arrival in Calais. On October 22nd, Husee was writing 'men looketh for the coming of the Queen, but no man knoweth the time certain'. Two days later, he wrote that officers had been chosen to go over to Calais to prepare for the visit, but again there was no fixed date 'Howbeit, when they depart is yet uncertain, yet some thinketh within six or seven days'. On November 14th, Husee was still writing to say that the day of her arrival was still unknown. The only certain piece of information that he sent told Lisle that the King would greet Anne at Blackheath, not at Canterbury. All the time, Lisle was hoping that he might accompany the new Queen to England but Husee informed him that, in spite of representations to Cromwell, Lisle's duty lay in Calais, where he would conduct her to the 'water's edge' and then take his leave. However, in his capacity as resident deputy in Calais, Cromwell sent further orders to him that he and the Lord Admiral, accompanied by men-at-arms and officials of the town, should meet Anne at the border of the English garrison town. Cromwell was determined that Anne and her retinue should be made truly welcome and sent the following orders to the officials as Calais that they should go forward,

> in their best array, (to) meet and receive her Grace at her entry into the English pale and, after their due reverence and salutations made to her, they shall conduct her and her train to the town, making all honest and friendly semblance and entertainment, whereby they may perceive themselves most heartily welcome.

A similar reception was arranged for her when she arrived in England. The plans for Anne's journey and the receptions for her show the scale of Cromwell's powers of organization and the lavishness of the occasions. He decided who was to accompany the King; how many servants they could bring; what clothes they should wear; he ordered ships and arranged payments for wages and accommodation. As well as organizing people, he arranged for suitable royal gold and silver dishes and equipment to be ready in Calais, Dover and Canterbury for the festivities. In addition, special work was carried out on the former monastic buildings at Canterbury, Rochester and Dartford, to make them suitable for a future Queen of England. Two of the King's beds were sent, one to Rochester and one to Dartford, to be ready there 'for the Queen's Grace'.

Directions to Christopher More of Loseley in Surrey provide an example of Cromwell's meticulous administrative skills: More was to be a member of the guard of honour to meet Anne when she arrived at Dover. He was required to be ready for service in London on December 10th, with six 'honestly furnished servants', and dressed in a coat of black velvet, with a gold chain around his neck and have a gown of velvet 'or other good silk' for a change of clothes. Similar orders went out to more than 200 knights and esquires. Cromwell's plans to ensure a smooth journey for her extended to issuing orders to local officials to clear and clean the streets all along her route from Dover to Greenwich. He had the streets of Greenwich widened, cleared and laid with gravel; he ordered James Needham, the King's surveyor and master carpenter, to build barriers along the river Thames, in case the crowds would be 'put in danger of drowning'.

Marillac wrote that on November 14th the King had gone to Hampton Court to wait for news of Anne's arrival. On the last day of November he reported that the courier, who had been sent to Cleves to find out the details of Anne's journey, had returned, bringing letters to say that she would be at Calais on December 8th. She travelled throughout the journey in a carriage which the chronicler described as 'well-carved and gilt with the arms of her country curiously wrought and covered with cloth of gold'. The programme for her journey still exists and shows that she left Dusseldorf at the beginning of October and travelled slowly, stopping in such towns as Cleves, Berg, Antwerp, Bruges and Dunkirk on her way to Calais. She proceeded with great pomp and ceremony, being escorted by almost 300 attendants; the costs of such a journey were met by her brother.

Anne's reception at Antwerp had been planned by Cromwell. It was a city that he had visited in his earlier days as a young businessman since it contained a large contingent of English merchants and an English trading-house. When she was approaching the city, the English merchants, dressed in velvet coats with chains of gold, went out to meet their future Queen; they accompanied her to her lodgings and entertained her at their trading-house. Wootton, who travelled in the procession, reported to Cromwell that the city was crowded with people who had come to see her. He commented 'it was a goodly sight'. The next day the merchants rode part of the way with her to Stetkyn and so she continued her journey. Her entourage travelled slowly, sometimes at the rate of only five miles a day, and she was delayed at the river Schelde because low water made it difficult to convey the horses across. Eventually, she arrived at the pale of Calais on December 11th, early in the morning, just a few days later than planned.[5]

A splendid reception awaited Anne at Calais as she first set foot on English soil. Calais had been captured for the English by Edward III in 1347 after a long siege. The town was then settled by English people and remained an important fortress until 1558, when it was recaptured by the French. For over 200 years, it gave the English easy access to France and it was considered to be one of the most important English towns. Edward III had made the town the staple, or market, for wool, leather, tin and lead; these were then the four main commodities for which there was a foreign market. During the fifteenth century, the wool trade became pre-eminent and Calais was the only point of entry for English exports to the continent. The staplers, who managed the trade, received all the market tolls and customs dues in return for the upkeep of the fortifications of the town and a garrison force. By the sixteenth century, the importance of the staplers had declined and this affected the status of the town itself. Gradually, the English ceased to be in the majority and the town lost its English character. The surrounding area, covering about 120 square miles, lay within a boundary known as the English pale. Marin Sanuto, a Venetian envoy who sent back reports to the senate in Venice and kept a diary of his travels, gave a firsthand account of Calais in 1531 as a 'very strong place, and very closely guarded by the most serene King of England.' This was the first English town to welcome Anne of Cleves. Thomas Cromwell had sent his son, Gregory, to be part of the welcoming committee. As a sign of his father's ambitions for the family, Gregory was married to Elizabeth Seymour, the sister of Queen Jane. He was already in Calais and he wrote to his wife on December 9th:

> Anne will be here on Thursday next. She will cross (the channel) on Sunday, depending on wind and weather. Lord Lisle and his officers will receive her at the pale, my Lord

Admiral with all of us, a little without the town, Lady Lisle and other ladies at the town gate.

As Gregory Cromwell recorded, she was met first by Lord Lisle, in his capacity as governor of Calais and Henry's representative there, and by various officials of the town. The next group, led by the Earl of Southampton and other English lords and gentlemen, met her outside the town in splendid array; Southampton was dressed in purple and cloth of gold, with gold fastenings and a gold chain. Three hundred men of the royal household were richly dressed 'with gold and massy chains', Sir Francis Bryan and Sir Thomas Seymour were especially conspicuous since they were wearing chains 'of great value and strange fashion'. As well as these, Southampton brought a large number of gentlemen, grandly dressed in blue velvet and crimson satin. His yeomen and his sailors wore the same colours, but in damask and Bruges satin. These all greeted their future Queen outside the town and accompanied Anne and her retinue to Calais, bringing her to the Lantern Gate, which was the main gate of the town, leading to the market-place. At the gate, she was welcomed by Lady Lisle and other noble ladies.

As she entered the town, all the English ships in the harbour, richly decorated with silk and gold banners, fired a salute of welcome. In particular, two of the royal ships, the *Lion* and the *Sweepstakes*, were dressed with 100 banners of gold and silk and, at Anne's arrival, their crews of master-gunners, mariners, trumpeters and drummers, fired 150 rounds of ammunition as a greeting. Their combined action produced so much smoke that people lost sight of one another in the darkness of the late December day. On her entry, the King's soldiers, the officials and mayor of Calais, the common people and the English merchants of the Staple lined the streets along the way to her lodgings. When she reached the place where she was staying, the mayor and his councillors presented her with 50 gold sovereigns and the mayor of the Staple gave her 60 gold sovereigns. Her lodgings were at a house called the 'Checker', or the 'Exchequer', which was known as 'the King's place' and had been made ready for her on the orders of Cromwell. The following day, entertainments were organized for her—there were tournaments, banquets and all other kinds of entertainment that a royal garrison could be expected to provide for their Queen.

Anne's retinue of 263 attendants was led by the Earl of Overstein and by Sir John Dulzike, who was the marshall of the Duke of Saxony. She was also accompanied by Olisleger, who acted as her interpreter, by her steward, by Lord Pallant and his younger brother (described by Wootton as 'jolly fellows both') and various other gentlemen and their servants, all from Cleves. Her ladies were headed by Mrs Gilmyn, an English widow, who had been sent by Henry to Cleves in October to help Anne prepare for her life in England. The rest of her ladies were from Cleves and included Lady Keteler, Lady Wyssem and Lady Pallant. In addition to these, there were five young gentlewomen who were companions for her and three other gentlewomen as servants.

Southampton sent the following report to inform Henry about Anne's arrival and the entertainment provided for her. He described a successful day:

> Yesterday, when my Lady's Grace had dined, I brought her to the Lantern Gate where her Grace saw as well the ship that is prepared for her passage as other of your Grace's ships, which were not only right well appointed and trimmed with streamers, banners and flags, but also no less furnished with men standing in their tops, the shrouds, the yard-arms and other places. And surely not only she, but also all such strangers as were with her much commend and liked the same.

Because of the bad weather, Anne's journey to England had to be delayed and she remained in Calais for over two weeks—'for want of a prosperous wind'. In view of the uncertain weather, Southampton had organized a warning system so that, as soon as the weather cleared, they would be able to set sail. He arranged for trumpeters to give a signal to all to be ready and Anne co-operated by agreeing 'always to be ready to go'. There was clearly no shortage of trumpeters, since the Duke of Saxony had sent 13 trumpeters and two drummers, with their instruments, who played before Anne on her entry to Calais and wished to travel to England. Since Anne seemed to want this as well, Southampton agreed to take the extra passengers. To while away the time, she asked through her interpreter to be taught a game of cards that Henry liked to play and she happily played the game of 'cent' or 'sent' with Southampton. (Sent resembles piquet, a game in which one side scores 30 points before the other side scores at all). Southampton reported the details of the meeting to Henry:

> And having this holy day not being with my Lady, this afternoon I went to her Grace to visit and salute the same and to know her pleasure. After much communication, she prayed me by Olisleger (her interpreter) to go to cards at some game that your Highness used, to the intent she might learn. And so my Lord William (Howard) and I played with her at cent and Mr Morison, Mrs Gilmyn and Mr Wooton stood by and taught her the play. And I assure your Majesty she played as pleasantly and with as good a grace and countenance as ever in all my life I saw any noble woman.

To keep up her spirits and perhaps calm her fears, Anne also asked Southampton to come to supper and bring other English noblemen with him to entertain her. He was cautious about accepting such an invitation, since this was not an English custom and Henry might not approve. However, Anne convinced him that it was usual in her country, and Southampton did as she wished, accompanied by the Lords Howard, Hastings, Grey and Talbot, and Mr Bryan, Mr Seymour and Mr Knevet, together with Gregory Cromwell–'Mr Morison should have set there, but there lacked room'. Southampton obviously enjoyed the evening and showed his pleasure by his favourable comments to Cromwell that 'her manner was like a Princess'. The English at Calais were keen to promote their own interests and gain the favour of the new Queen at an early stage. Anne's period of waiting gave them an unexpected chance to make a good impression. As soon as they heard that Anne was to be at Calais, Lord and Lady Lisle's friends had rushed to offer to help with her reception. One offered a boar's head, expressing his sorrow that he had nothing better to give, while another offered a second boar's head and a mule 'enharnessed for your service when that the Queen of England shall come to Calais'. Conspicuous among those looking for patronage was her hostess, Lady Lisle. She took advantage of Anne's prolonged stay to recommend her daughters by her previous marriage, Anne and Katherine Basset. Anne Basset, the elder daughter, had been a maid of honour to Jane Seymour. Although she had no official position after Jane's death, she seems to have had a stipend and was a member of the royal household. The King enjoyed her company and in August she had travelled with other ladies of the Queen's privy chamber on a visit to Portsmouth to see his ships in the harbour there. In addition, Henry had given her a present of a horse and a saddle to go with it. She enjoyed her life at court and she was clearly hoping to be maid of honour to Anne of Cleves.

Anne Basset wrote excitedly from England to her mother about the eagerness in England for the new Queen and all the prospects for favours and patronage. As well as promoting the interests of her eldest daughter, Lady Lisle, was also keen to have her second daughter, Katherine, appointed maid of honour to Anne of Cleves. As early as October, Katherine had written to her mother saying that she had heard of the coming royal wedding and she urged Lady Lisle to use her influence to make her maid of honour to Anne:

> Wherefore I desire your ladyship that ye will be so good lady and mother unto me as to speak that I may be one of the Queen's maids; for I have no trust in none other but your ladyship to speak for me in that cause.

For this purpose, Lady Lisle wrote letters and sent presents to powerful friends at Henry's court, hoping to gain their favour and support. Not content with trying to influence the leading courtiers, Lady Lisle took advantage of the King's well-known liking for sweet dishes and sent him delicacies of her own making, marmalade and jam. Anne Basset wrote to her mother that the King had enjoyed them so much and 'his Grace commanded me to write to you for more of the quince marmalade of the clearest making and damson conserve; and this as soon as may be.'

Anne Basset's reply throws some light on Lady Lisle's opinions of the future Queen. Anne wrote to her mother:

> I humbly thank your ladyship of the news you write me of her Grace, that she is good and gentle to serve and please. It shall be no little rejoicement to us her Grace's servants here that

shall attend daily upon her, and most comfort to the King's majesty, whose highness is not a little desirous to have her Grace here.[1]

But Anne of Cleves, not knowing the customs of the English court, had already appointed young women of Cleves as her maids of honour, and there were no chances for young English women to take this role. While the highest offices in her household were reserved for English royal ladies, Anne sensibly ensured that she had some familiar companions of her own age who could speak her language.

The Lisles were hoping to gain an advantage by entertaining Anne well at Calais, so that they might accompany the new Queen on the next stage of her journey and be well-placed in England. Anne Basset also had the same hopes and she had written that she expected to see them soon in England, but Lisle was ordered to stay at Calais and Lady Lisle loyally remained with him. In the event, the reception of Anne of Cleves had brought the Lisles only extra expenses and responsibilities, without any apparent reward. Katherine Basset too, failed to become maid of honour to the Queen and, for the time being at least, she remained in the household of Lady Rutland.

The weather in the English Channel was so stormy that Anne was forced to stay in Calais for Christmas, where she was entertained by the Lisles. It was not until December 27th that she was eventually able to sail. She left Calais at about midday with a convoy of 50 ships; by this time, the weather was so good that the crossing took only six or seven hours and she landed near Deal later the same day. On her arrival, she was welcomed by Sir Thomas Cheney, Lord Warden of the Cinque Ports, and she stayed for a while at Deal Castle. This was the largest of a group of three forts: Deal, Sandown and Walmer, sometimes known as the Castles in the Downs, that had been recently built along the Kent coast in 1538 as a protection against the threat of invasion by the French. The work on Deal Castle had only begun in April but, in spite of a strike by the workmen, who demanded wages of 6d a day, it must have been almost finished, since it was considered to be ready for Anne's visit. The fear of invasion had led to the construction of a series of coastal defences, batteries and low-lying castles from the Thames estuary as far as the Isles of Scilly. In fact, none of them was ever tested by enemy action, because of the superiority of the English fleet.

In Henry's new castle at Deal, the Duke and Duchess of Suffolk, the Bishop of Chichester, with a large retinue of knights and esquires, waited to welcome Anne and from there they escorted her to the safety and comfort of Dover Castle. In the past, the castle had been primarily a military establishment and during the earlier part of 1539 it was used as the administrative centre and supply base for building the new Kentish forts. But it was also a convenient stopping-place for royal travellers to and from France. There was a King's side and a Queen's side in the castle, both of which were suitably fitted out for royal visitors. It was the usual practice to carry out repairs and alterations in advance of such a visit. Needham's detailed pay-books for 1538-41 have not survived but certainly some work was done on the castle in 1539 before Anne arrived. They seem to have been mostly structural repairs to the outer walls and towers, not decorative. But perhaps some of the windows were tactfully replaced—some new ones had been installed during 1536 and bore the emblems of the former Queen, Jane Seymour. Anne rested at the castle for just one day and then, in spite of the wintry weather and heavy, driving rain, she kept to the plan for her journey. With a great retinue of attendants she set out for her next stopping-place at Canterbury, 15 miles distant.

As she travelled quickly from Dover towards London along Watling Street she was welcomed at Barham Down by Thomas Cranmer, Archbishop of Canterbury, and other bishops and gentlemen. They escorted her to the comfort of St Augustine's Abbey, which lay just outside the walls of the city of Canterbury. The abbey was founded by St Augustine in 597 and, until the martyrdom of Thomas Becket at Canterbury in 1170, it had been the greatest Benedictine house in England. But Becket's fate had promoted the fame of the cathedral and brought decline to the reputation of the abbey. The Venetian envoy, Sanuto, wrote an account of his visit to Canterbury in 1531 and revealed how impressive he found the cathedral. He wrote in his diary:

> The place is very famous by reason of the veneration for the glorious Saint Thomas, and there is a superb and magnificent shrine containing his tomb ornamented with precious stones and sundry jewels, with so much gold that its value is inestimable.

Although Becket's tomb attracted people to the cathedral, the buildings of St Augustine's Abbey still rivalled those of the cathedral in magnificence. However, the abbey had been dissolved in 1538 and it was rapidly converted into a royal palace.

While the dissolution of the monasteries provided Henry with a windfall of wealth, it also presented him with difficulties concerning accommodation. Before the dissolution, he had made extensive use of monastic buildings as lodgings in his travels around the country. Because royalty regularly stayed at such places, lodgings were often set aside permanently for them and money was paid out of the royal accounts for their upkeep. In addition, many of these establishments lay conveniently close to the main roads which linked London with the ports of the south coast. Rather than lose these facilities, Henry took them over wholesale and made some of them into royal houses for regular use while travelling.

As soon as the marriage plans were announced, the King gave orders for parts of St Augustine's Abbey to be converted for royal use—'against the coming of the Lady Anne of Cleves'. Following Cromwell's instructions, Needham was busy there from October 5th (the day after the treaty was signed) until December 21st, making arrangements for fitting-up the apartments in suitable style for the future Queen. Clearly the work had to be carried out at speed and the bills for candles show that work must have continued during the hours of darkness. When the work was finished, charcoal was burned in the rooms to speed up the drying process and Needham was probably grateful for the bad weather which delayed Anne's arrival for a while. The former abbot's lodgings were converted into the King's apartments, without too much extra work. But there were no buildings that could readily be converted into apartments for the Queen. For these, Needham used the existing gatehouse, with the addition of a further range of brick and timber buildings. The King's and Queen's apartments were close together; the royal bedchambers were separated only by a 'little chamber betwixt the two'. The improved domestic comforts included items such as extra doorways, new fireplaces and bay windows. Galyon Hone, the King's glazier, marked the changes by installing decorative badges and coats of arms of the King and the new Queen in the windows. As an additional welcome to the new Queen, John Hethe of London painted four examples of her coat of arms in the Queen's apartments. The total cost of the work was about £650. The scale of the new buildings was clearly designed to make a good impression on the foreign visitors. All this work reflects Henry's original intention to meet Anne at Canterbury, in a setting that would have been suitably impressive for the occasion. Following all these changes, no later additions needed to be made to the buildings although St Augustine's Abbey continued in use as a royal residence and later members of the royal family stayed there, including Elizabeth I, Charles I and Charles II.

Everything went well at Canterbury. Cheney and Suffolk recorded the reception given to Anne of Cleves there and wrote to Cromwell that:

> The mayor and citizens received her with torchlight and a good peal of guns. In her chamber (there) were 40 or 50 gentlewomen in velvet bonnets to see her, all which she took very joyously, and was so glad to see the King's subjects resorting so lovingly to her that she forgot all the foul weather and was very merry at supper.

Coincidentally, on this part of her journey, she was following the same route which the Emperor Charles V had taken in 1520 on his brief visit to England.[1]

The next day she travelled to Sittingbourne, where again she stayed the night. By this time, she was about 40 miles from London. There was no obvious royal residence at Sittingbourne; Leland's *Itinerary*, which gives a contemporary description of the town, mentions only the main street–'a pretty thoroughfare of one parish', named after the bourne or stream that runs through it. Sittingbourne was a regular staging-post on the main route from London to Dover and there were plenty of inns in the town for travellers to stay at. Certainly, when the King visited the town in 1532, there was a payment to the 'wif of the Lyon', who was presumably the landlady of the local inn. There were also several fairly large private houses in the vicinity, but perhaps they were too small to provide adequate accommodation for all the visitors in 1539–Cheney and Suffolk described it as 'not a place to stay long'–and they hurried Anne on to the next stage of the journey. The following day was New Year's Eve and Anne set out again, being met at Rainham by a further retinue led by Thomas Howard, Duke of Norfolk, Lord Mountjoy and Lord Dacre, in company with other lords, knights and esquires, all dressed in velvet adorned with chains of gold. This splendid escort accompanied her to Rochester where she stayed at the bishop's palace and spent New Year's Day.[2]

In contrast to the simplicity of Sittingbourne, Rochester was the second cathedral city of Kent after Canterbury. It stands on the river Medway and once occupied a strategic position at the lowest point where the river could be bridged. It lies where Watling Street crosses the Medway and so it commanded the main overland route from London to Canterbury and Dover. The Norman castle and the cathedral dominated the town, which was a seat for bishops and a staging-post for royalty. By the sixteenth century, the castle was in a state of decay and was no longer suitable for royal visitors. Like St Augustine's Abbey at Canterbury, Rochester Cathedral was also a Benedictine foundation.

But, unlike St Augustine's, there was less repair work hurriedly carried out at Rochester. Perhaps the palace was already in good order. Certainly, in 1459, John Lowe, the Bishop of Rochester, remodelled and enlarged the palace, calling it his 'new palace in Rochester'. However, when Erasmus visited Bishop John Fisher there, he made disapproving remarks about the palace because it was too near a tidal river and he considered that the windows allowed in unwholesome air. In 1534, after Fisher had been committed to the Tower, an inventory of the palace listed the chambers, several studies, chapels, various galleries, parlour and the service quarters, including the kitchen and brew-house. The arrangement of the rooms suggests that they lay on three sides of a central courtyard, with the bishop's garden at the rear. Wolsey stayed at the palace in 1527 while on his way to France and, in a letter to the King he described himself as lovingly and kindly entertained by Fisher. At the time, Wolsey was accompanied by a retinue of about 100 nobles and gentlemen, together with their servants, many of whom had to be lodged in the city. The bishop's palace, where Anne was entertained, lay between the castle and cathedral. Parts of the palace still remain, now incorporated into later buildings.[3]

Lists of the King's payments for the year 1540 give some clues about the scale of her reception that was everywhere prepared for her. There were wages for 28 yeomen of the guard, 'being no daily waiters, but sent for by the King's commandment to give their attendance at the Queen's coming into this realm from December 10th until January 19th'. Extensive payments were made to members of the royal household for their work in anticipation of Anne's visit. For example, John Norris and William Morris were paid for working for a total of 41 days at Calais, preparing the Queen's lodgings there. Others were paid for up to 35 days spent in 'making ready at Dover, Canterbury, Sittingbourne, Rochester and Dartford against the Queen's coming'.[4]

John Norris, who had stayed on at Calais to be an escort to Anne of Cleves, wrote to Lady Lisle, giving his version of Anne's journey through Kent, which again emphasized the speed of travel, in spite of bad weather, and the warm welcome that Anne received wherever she travelled. After staying at Dover on Sunday, he reported that she went on to Canterbury on Monday, where she was received outside the city by the archbishop. As at Calais and at other towns on the continent, it was customary to receive important guests outside the town and escort them in. The same ceremonial welcome took place in England:

> Three miles from Canterbury there met with her Grace my Lord of Canterbury with three hundred gentlemen, and at Canterbury in her Grace's Great Chamber there stood four (score) more ladies and gentlewomen. The next day, which was Tuesday, her Grace went to Sittingbourne, and stayed there that night. Upon Wednesday to Rochester, my Lord of Norfolk with an hundred horses and a goodly company of gentlemen in (–) velvet and chains about their necks; and so lay there New Year's Day.[5]

The enthusiastic reception and welcome given to Anne everywhere she went suggests that people were glad to have a new Queen and were looking forward to a return to cheerfulness after a rather dismal two years without a royal first lady.

Henry had changed his earlier plan to meet Anne at St Augustine's Abbey at Canterbury and he stayed in London instead. He was not due to see his new bride until the first formal meeting at Greenwich on January 3rd, but he could not control his desire to see her and he set out eagerly for Rochester on New Year's Day. He and several gentlemen of the Kings' Privy Chamber rode in disguise in clothes of varied colours–'all apparelled in marble coats' said the chronicler–aiming to provide the new Queen with a delightful surprise. By the afternoon they reached Rochester, where Henry was anticipating a joyful and loving meeting.

There are various versions of the encounter; some say that Henry sent Sir Anthony Browne ahead to announce the visit. Browne afterwards described his own reaction at seeing Anne, being 'struck with consternation when he was shown the Queen, and was never so much dismayed in his life as to see a lady so far unlike what had been represented'. Out of deference to the King's judgement, he made no comment and let Henry see her for himself. When Henry finally met Anne, his high hopes of finding love and affection were totally dashed; he was bitterly disappointed at her appearance. Lord Russell was present at the meeting and later declared that 'he never saw his highness so marvellously astonished and abashed as on that occasion'. Anne's reaction was probably one of equal surprise, since she was suddenly and unexpectedly confronted with a man who was twice her age, ungainly, moody and bad-tempered because of his painfully swollen leg. However, according to the account in Hall's chronicle, she reacted calmly by offering him a loving greeting; in return, Henry kissed her and stayed until evening.[1]

Wriothesley's version of events was slightly different. He said that she happened to be looking out of a window watching a game of bull-baiting in the courtyard below when Henry arrived in disguise. Because he was in disguise, she took very little notice of him. Only when she saw him in splendid clothes and all the lords bowing to him, did she realize who he was. According to Wriothesley, the two then spent the evening pleasantly together.[2] Other accounts say the sound of her voice was so harsh that Henry found it unbearable and would not even use an interpreter to communicate with her.

Six months later Cromwell gave his version of events, saying that when he asked the King what he thought of Anne, Henry replied 'nothing as well as she was spoken of and, if he had known so much before, she would not have come'. Whatever happened at the first meeting, Henry was clearly very upset. He quickly left her company and called for the lords who had brought her from Calais, deeply angry because he had been so much misled. He questioned Southampton, asking why he had sent good reports of her from Calais. 'Do you think her so personable, fair and beautiful as reported?' Southampton diplomatically replied 'I take her not for fair but to be of a brown complexion'. The King showed his distrust and asked why he had received only good reports of her—'I am ashamed that men have praised her as they have done, and I like her not'. Southampton was in a difficult situation: he had been forced to balance the King's likely displeasure at the risk of offending his future Queen. The other officials must have been faced with a similar dilemma to which there was no happy outcome. Anne was then aged 24, which compared favourably with Jane Seymour, who was 25 when she married Henry. Similar to Anne, Jane had not been particularly beautiful; she was rather pale and was not outstanding in appearance or accomplishments. But in spite of her fairly ordinary looks, she must have appeared attractive to Henry in a way that Anne could not match. Most commentators agree that Anne looked older than 24, was fairly tall, had a calm, unassuming disposition, and wore the kind of clothes that were then quite unfashionable in England and France. She was not young, or lively, or appealing, in a way that would stir Henry's feelings.

The disappointed King did not have the heart to make a personal New Year's gift to Anne and the next day he sent Sir Anthony Browne to present her with his gift of rich sable furs. Henry stayed at Greenwich, unhappy at the prospect of having to go through with the marriage. He reacted angrily by attacking Cromwell for providing him with such a wife. While there is no direct evidence for his complaint that he had been presented with 'a great Flanders mare', these words reflected his attitude to Anne and have become accepted as historical fact. For example, Smollett's *History of England*, published in 1759, stated 'The King found her so different from her picture that he swore that they had brought him a Flanders mare'.[3] Cromwell responded to Henry's views by turning on Southampton, criticizing him for bringing Anne to England. But he replied that 'as the Princess was generally reported for a beauty, he had only repeated the opinions of others; for which no-one ought to blame him, especially as he supposed she would be his Queen'.[4] Among these bitter mutual recriminations, the King then demanded a way out of the marriage. In the meantime, Anne continued on her journey and followed the Dover road from Rochester to Dartford, which lies about 14 miles from London. At Dartford she stayed at another royal residence on the site of a former Dominican priory, which Henry had taken over to use as royal lodgings. This was a place to which she would return in her later years.

VIII   Wedding

The French ambassador, Marillac, sent his version of events associated with the wedding to Francis I. He wrote on January 5th 1540 saying that a proclamation was made by the public crier in London and Greenwich on January 2nd that all who loved the King should go to Greenwich to welcome Anne of Cleves, the future Queen of England. Both Marillac and Eustace Chapuys, the Spanish ambassador, were invited to the reception. Marillac reported that Anne's welcome was the most imposing and honourable that could be imagined—probably as a result of Cromwell's meticulous planning. The noblemen and gentlemen on horseback were to be in their places near the pale of Greenwich Park by 8 am on the cold January morning. Cromwell's plan had allowed for a postponement in the event of 'extreme weather', but fortunately, it was a fine day. Marillac referred to the welcome that she received, 'which was well conducted with marvellous silence and no confusion'—even though between 5000 and 6000 horses were present. The Dukes of Norfolk and Suffolk escorted her from Dartford towards Greenwich, while the King, with the rest of his household, went out to meet her at Blackheath. Marillac went on to make further comments about Anne, none of them flattering; he described her as 'clothed in the fashion of the country from which she came' and he reflected on her appearance, saying that she looked about thirty years of age, tall and thin, of middling beauty, with a determined and resolute expression.

In his letter to the High Constable of France, the ambassador gave more details about Anne's appearance. He wrote that, on closer inspection, she looked older than 24 and was not as beautiful as everyone expected. Again he mentioned her height, her assurance, and her steady and determined expression but, like Wootton, he hinted at her intelligence, saying that she showed a turn of mind and vivacity of wit that counterbalanced her lack of beauty. He made a further comment on her maids of honour who were not only inferior to her in beauty, but dressed in such outlandish clothes 'so heavily and unbecomingly' that, even if they had been beautiful, the clothes made them appear ugly.[1] Her rather elderly looks, her height and her strange clothes aroused most criticism; obviously, her personality caused less concern to the observers. The portraits of Anne support Marillac's comments—we see a face that is not particularly beautiful, but calm and determined. Her face is overwhelmed by her clothes, which were lavishly embroidered with exquisite needlework and decorated with jewels. Holbein shows a delicate, transparent veil around her face and a superb dress with massively wide shoulders, all of which made a splendid impression, but were out of fashion in England in 1540. Contemporary portraits show that noble English women of the time were wearing light, five-pointed hats, which revealed their faces. Their dresses had plainer bodices, with low-cut necklines, forming a complete contrast with Anne's elaborate clothes.

Hall's chronicle gives more details about the first formal meeting between Anne and Henry. On January 3rd at Blackheath, near the foot of Shooters Hill, magnificent tents and pavilions, warmed and perfumed, were pitched for Anne and her ladies. The road from the tents to the gate of Greenwich Park had been cleared of bushes and trees to make a fine processional way to the palace and to provide plenty of room for welcoming officials. The merchants of the Steelyard stood next to the park pale on the east side, while the Italian and Spanish merchants, dressed in velvet coats, stood on the western side. About 160 merchants of the City of London, aldermen and members of the city council lined the route. Next came the knights, then 50 gentlemen pensioners—all dressed in velvet with gold chains—and behind them were placed the King's men on horseback. The retinues of Cromwell and Southampton and all the other lords were close by, dressed in similar splendour. The people of London played their part in the welcome. They were rowing up and down the Thames and every craft was decorated with banners. One of the barges, called 'the bachelors' bark', had equipment for shooting 'great pieces of artillery', while many others had a store of musical instruments and men and women were singing and playing music as the King and Queen passed by.

At about twelve noon Anne and all her companions from Cleves, together with the Dukes of Norfolk and Suffolk, the Archbishop of Canterbury and other bishops, lords and knights, rode towards the royal tents. Before she reached them, she was welcomed by the Earl of Rutland, who was to be her chamberlain, Sir Thomas Dennys, her chancellor, and all her English officials. Her almoner, Dr Kaye, presented all the new officers of her household to her with a speech in Latin. A representative of the Duke of Cleves made a formal reply. Then all her English ladies were presented to her. These were headed by Lady Margaret Douglas and Lady Francis Dorset, nieces of the King, and were accompanied by the Duchess of Richmond and the Countesses of Rutland and Hertford, with various other ladies, making a total of about 65 women. She left her coach and thanked and kissed them all. Finally, she and her ladies went into the tents and enjoyed the warmth there.

When the King knew that she had reached her tent, he set out from Greenwich Palace through the park to meet her. His officials and members of his household went first, all richly dressed, mostly in purple velvet, and riding on magnificent horses. Henry was also dressed in purple velvet, with gold embroidery and buttons of diamonds, rubies and pearls. His sword belt and his hat were similarly splendid with glittering jewels and pearls. He was attended by his lord chamberlain, by Sir Anthony Browne, master of horse, and by Sir Anthony Wingfield, captain of the guard, who was leading the King's guard.

Anne came out of her tent to greet the King. She was dressed in a rich gown of cloth of gold, her face was veiled, she wore a round bonnet set with pearls and a coronet of black velvet. At the door of her tent, she mounted her horse and, accompanied by her footmen, rode towards the King. The two of them then rode together to Greenwich. A great procession of all the lords and ladies of both households went with them to Greenwich Palace. It was a suitable setting for such a splendid occasion. The palace, built by Henry VII, had a magnificent frontage, with the bay windows of the King's apartments overlooking the Thames. Greenwich had been the scene of many grand occasions during the earlier years of Henry VIII. While Jane Seymour was Queen, work had been done on the King's apartments, when magnificent ceilings were installed, all gilded and moulded, showing the arms of Henry and Jane. In addition, the great bay windows had been decorated with emblems of the King and Queen. The Queen's rooms similarly had gilded ceilings and were paved with expensive syvyll (Seville) tiles or cheaper yellow and green Flanders tiles. In 1539, the Queen's private apartments had been richly and lavishly refurnished especially for Anne of Cleves. After the royal procession entered the palace, Anne went to the Queen's apartments and she stayed there until the day of the wedding on January 6th.[2] Anne's reception at Greenwich proved to be the last great public spectacle of Henry's reign.

Henry was still anxious to find a way out of the marriage and questioned Cromwell again about Anne's pre-contract with Francis of Lorraine. The King called a meeting of his counsellors to discuss ways of discrediting the marriage plans without upsetting the Duke of Cleves or changing the pattern of alliances with Cleves and the Protestant states. The Duke of Cleves' envoys, Overstein and Olisleger, were suddenly confronted with a quite unexpected diplomatic problem. They were ordered by the council to provide conclusive evidence that the pre-contract was truly dissolved. Since they had no written proof of the annulment, they tried to use delaying tactics by saying that it would take about three months to provide a copy from the chancery office in Cleves. In their embarrassment and confusion, the two men felt obliged to offer themselves as hostages until the certificate of annulment arrived. To try to resolve the question, Anne was made to swear before the counsellors and lawyers that she was free of any contract. Cromwell later quoted the King's words on this occasion when Henry sadly declared:

> If it were not that she is come so far into my realm and the great preparations that my states and my people have made for her and for fear of making a ruffle in the world—that is to mean to drive her brother into the hands of the Emperor and the French King's hands, being now together, I would never have her, but now it is so far gone.

Opinions among the King's advisers were divided: Cranmer and the Bishop of Durham considered that the marriage with Anne would be lawful, while others put the view that, if Anne should have any children, a marriage of dubious legality would cause problems later for the succession in England. In addition, Cromwell's hopes of ensuring a balance of power in Europe through links with Cleves would be in danger if the marriage was abandoned. Finally, Henry unwillingly agreed, saying 'is there then no remedy, but that I must needs put my neck into the yoke'.[3]

There was no going back. On the day before the wedding, the letters patent were drawn up, granting Anne 'annuities, honors, castles and manors in various counties; to be held in as ample a manner as Jane, late Queen of England, held the same'. As part of the settlement she received the property of the dissolved priory of St Margaret, near Marlborough, in Wiltshire, the property of the former priories of Southwick and Breamore in Hampshire, and various manors in Essex. Although Anne was in no way involved in the dissolution of the monasteries, it is easy to see how these grants of former monastic lands caused the general public to form a link between her arrival and the changes brought about by the reformation. The grant of Southwick priory to Anne provides a good example of such a perceived connection. The wholesale removal of images and pilgrimage saints from churches had led John Borough to write to Lisle in Calais. He specifically mentioned Southwick, saying that he had heard that 'Our Lady of Southwick was taken down and the priory is to be suppressed'. Husee similarly wrote sadly to Lisle about Southwick–'pilgrimage saints goeth down apace'.[4]

After Henry's reluctant acquiescence, the wedding was arranged for 8 am the following morning. But, while the King was duly making his preparations for the ceremony, there were doubts about who should be leading Anne to the ceremony. Officially, the Earls of Essex and Overstein had been appointed for the honour, but Essex had failed to arrive in time. In the confusion, Cromwell was ordered to lead her, but Essex finally arrived and he was joined by Anne's compatriot, Overstein. Hall described Henry's appearance–he wore a gown of cloth of gold embroidered with great flowers of silver and decorated with fur. His crimson coat was slashed and embroidered and fastened with diamonds and he wore a rich collar around his neck. The King's splendid appearance concealed his great unhappiness. Before the ceremony he summoned Cromwell and said gloomily 'My lord, if it were not to satisfy the world and my realm, I would not do what I must do this day for any earthly thing'.[5]

Then the bride was ready. She wore a dress of cloth of gold, embroidered with pearls, her hair was loose and flowing, which Hall described as fair, yellow and long, in contrast to her portraits which seem to show her with dark hair. She wore a gold coronet and had great jewels around her neck and waist. Her face was calm and demure. Accompanied by Essex and Overstein and a retinue of nobles, she went to meet Henry. Thomas Cranmer, Archbishop of Canterbury, performed the ceremony, Overstein gave her away and her wedding ring bore the inscription 'God send me well to keep'.

When the wedding ceremony was over, the bride and groom heard mass and then took wine and spices. The King and Queen went briefly to their separate apartments and later met for another service of the mass. They took dinner together and after dinner Anne changed into a gown 'like a man's gown' says Hall, with long, tight sleeves and sable fur. On her head she wore fine linen, richly decorated with pearls and jewels. Her ladies were dressed in similar fashion. Anne and Henry went to evensong and then took supper together. The day ended with banquets, and various entertainments until the King and Queen went to bed.

IX   After the Wedding

The next morning Cromwell found the King in a decidedly bad mood. When he enquired how Henry liked the Queen, the King replied 'Surely, my lord, as you know, I liked her before not well, but now I like her much worse'. He said later that he had felt her belly and breasts and had come to the conclusion that she was not a virgin, 'which when I felt them, struck me so to the heart that (I had) neither will nor courage to prove the rest'—he was so down-hearted that he could not bear to make love to her.[1]

The first few days of January must have presented Henry with a totally unexpected situation. From the first moment he saw Anne, there was no sexual chemistry—she had no power to attract him and he was not interested enough in her to take the trouble to stir her emotions. He had a strong sexual appetite and he assumed that his partners would be the same—he had probably never encountered a woman who seemed to be indifferent to his attractions. Unlike Anne Boleyn and Jane Seymour, she had no previous experience of English court life, nor were there any courtiers to advise her beforehand and give her lessons on how to anticipate Henry's wishes. Mrs Gilmyn's tuition at Cleves had probably covered manners and perhaps language, but not coquettish or sexual behaviour. Their marriage was characterized by a total lack of passion; they could be friends but not lovers. Although he suggested she was not a virgin before the wedding, her failure to show any emotional response to him and her strict upbringing make it unlikely that she ever had any previous lovers. Probably because of her lack of sexual experience she made no effort to pretend to feel affectionate towards him, whereas Henry, at the age of 49, was looking for excitement and stimulus—a need which quickly drove him into the welcoming arms of Catherine Howard. On the other hand, Anne had never seen Henry before and she was suddenly confronted with a husband who was twice her age, fat and ungainly. It is not surprising that she failed to respond to him in an emotional way. Sadly, the honeymoon was over before it had even begun. Cromwell, who had been so successful at carrying out the King's wishes in the past, had made a gigantic miscalculation and misjudgement which later cost him his life.

In spite of Henry's obvious unhappiness, his reactions were kept from public knowledge and the elaborate wedding celebrations continued. There were tournaments and jousting to entertain the visitors from Cleves. Anne attended these displays, dressed now in the English style and wearing a fashionable French hood instead of her strange German clothes, which had caused so much comment on her first appearance. Greenwich Palace was ideally suited to such entertainments. It had been the main royal palace for the first twenty years of Henry's reign and, in imitation of French customs, jousting and tournaments had become a regular activity of Henry's court. Sir Henry Courtney's household accounts, which were compiled twenty years earlier, in 1519, described the activities of the court at Greenwich during the winter. The courtiers spent their time out of doors engaged in jousting and throwing snowballs, watching bear- or bull-baiting, or even boar-hunting in the courtyards, while their indoor pastimes included playing tennis and shuffle-board. Because of his passion for all kinds of sporting activities, Henry had added tiltyards and stables to the palace. Tall tiltyard towers were built, linked by wooden galleries which provided a covered viewing space for the audience. Such structures were in frequent use and, in 1540, Thomas Culpeper received a payment of £16 13s 4d 'for keeping the gallery at Greenwich'. Permanent buildings like this allowed the court to enjoy tournaments and displays during the winter months. Such entertainments were part of the wedding celebrations to the delight of Anne and her compatriots. They were also now more suitable for Henry, whose bad leg forced him to be a passive spectator of events instead of taking an active part in them, as he had done in earlier years.

At the end of January, the Earl of Overstein and other lords and ladies, who had come with her from Cleves, made ready to return there, taking with them rich gifts in money and gold and silver plate, which they had received from the King. Morgan Wolf, the King's goldsmith, supplied gifts for the 'chief chancellor to the

Duke of Cleves and to the chief chancellor to the Duke of Bavaria', for them to take with them as leaving presents. Among the recipients of the gifts was Conrad Heresbach, the associate of Erasmus, and former tutor of William of Cleves, who had now become one of the Duke's advisers. Since various people from Cleves were now leaving, it became necessary to have English interpreters who could communicate with the Clevelanders who remained. Wymond Carew fulfilled this role. He had previously served in the household of Jane Seymour and he occasionally acted as an interpreter at court. It was Carew who negotiated payments to the visitors from Cleves and, in particular, 'to certain ladies, at their departing into Clevelande.' But some from Cleves stayed with Anne for company. Her maids of honour from Cleves were mocked by the English courtiers because of their voices and clothes and were usually referred to as 'the Dutch maids' or the 'strange maidens'. Lady Lisle failed in her attempt to have her daughters Anne and Katherine appointed as maids of honour to the Queen—she had tried to influence both Olisleger and Lady Rutland, but Mistress Lowe, 'the mother of the Dutch maids', was not sympathetic to such requests. Olisleger wrote to Lord Lisle acknowledging his failure to promote the interests of the two women, principally because, according to English custom, the appointments had already been made. He wrote as follows:

> My lord, very sorry at heart I am to advertise you that with the knowledge and goodwill of the Queen's Grace I have spoken with the King our master and also with my Lord Privy Seal and the other gentlemen of the Council, to have Mistress Katherine, your wife's daughter, to be of the Privy Chamber with the Queen.

Olisleger could only advise the Lisles to be patient and Katherine remained in the household of Lady Rutland, who was, in fact, a member of the Queen's household.[2]

In spite of Henry's protests to Cromwell, he kept up the appearance of marriage and seems to have stayed with her every night, or at least every other night. Anne later said that he greeted her with the words 'Good night, sweetheart' and said 'Farewell, darling', when he left her in the morning. The court remained at

Greenwich during January, enjoying the tournaments and other recreations. In February, the King and Queen travelled by royal barge in great state to Westminster, which was Anne's first appearance in London. One of the advantages of living at Greenwich was the ease and convenience of river travel from there to London. For this reason, wealthy people built their houses alongside the river and many of them, particularly the courtiers, chose to travel that way, rather than by road. But the gossips exaggerated and said that the King insisted on a journey by water to keep Anne out of sight of the general population, because he was so ashamed of the way she looked. However, even if the King had wished for such discretion, the merchants of the City of London were determined to put on a good show. The Lord Mayor and leading members of the city companies travelled by water in procession to accompany the royal barge. The merchants' barges were gloriously decorated with silk banners for the occasion, while other ships along the route fired welcoming salutes. When the procession reached the Tower of London, there was another salute of cannon fire. They reached Westminster by water and probably landed at Whitehall Palace. The King had taken over the large house in Westminster which was previously known as York House, since it had formerly been the London residence of the Archbishops of York. Wolsey had virtually rebuilt it while he held the office of Archbishop of York. By 1536 it was generally called the King's palace at Westminster. The Venetian envoy was deeply impressed with Henry's newly acquired palace. He wrote of the three so-called galleries, which were long porticos and halls, with windows on each side, looking out on to gardens and the river. The stone ceilings were decorated with gold, the wooden panelling was carved with 'a thousand beautiful figures'. All around there were rooms and very large halls, all hung with tapestries. To enhance the grandeur of the approach from the river, Henry had built a two-level landing stage, known as the Privy Bridge. It had a balustraded roof, like an additional gallery, from where courtiers could watch the pageants and displays which frequently took place on the river. This was the place where the King and Queen probably disembarked from the royal barges. It is now difficult for us to judge where the Queen's apartments lay. In the seventeenth century they faced the Thames and they may have been on the same site in the Tudor palace.[3]

After such a magnificent wedding and reception, people outside the court expected her coronation to follow fairly soon and were looking forward to another round of celebrations. No gossip about the marriage had reached the ears of the French or Spanish ambassadors—in March and again in April Marillac wrote to Francis I that Anne's coronation would take place towards the end of May. He referred to the preparations and eager anticipation of jousting, tournaments and entertainment that would occur at the coronation.[4]

The Queen's household was now established. Her council was headed by the Earl of Rutland, her chamberlain, Sir Thomas Dennys, her chancellor, and Sir John Dudley, the master of horse. She had about 100 male attendants, both gentlemen and yeomen, and about 30 females, led by Lady Margaret Douglas and the Duchesses of Richmond and Suffolk. Mrs Gilmyn, who had been sent by the King to attend Anne in Cleves before the wedding, remained in her household, and some of Anne's companions from Cleves stayed with her.[5] There were plenty of diversions for her court at Westminster. Henry had added a tiltyard for jousting and had put up buildings that were suitable for playing tennis and bowls and for watching cock-fighting.

Throughout this difficult time Henry seems to have treated her with courtesy. There is very little evidence for Anne's own reaction to the marriage, but her qualities of calmness, determination and strength of character helped to carry her through. Unfortunately, these same qualities of calm detachment and acceptance were not likely to arouse the interest of the King who liked to be entertained and stimulated by young and lively company. Because of the style of the ducal court at Cleves, Anne had never learned to sing or dance and, because of her ignorance of English, she could not amuse Henry with light-hearted conversation, as he may have expected. The rather modest tastes of the court of Cleves did not translate well to the sophisticated style of the English court. At first she could not understand English and perhaps she used her native wit and intelligence to read the expressions on the courtiers' faces until she understood the words they used. In a foreign country, where she did not know who she might trust, it may have taken some time before she fully realized the gulf between her and the King. At no time did she openly complain about Henry's attitude and Wootton wrote to Cromwell in February saying that Lady Keteler, when she left the Queen in England, was asked by Anne to thank her mother and brother in Cleves for agreeing to the marriage, as 'she could wish for no better'.[6]

Similarly, there are hardly any references to the public reaction to the new Queen. Henry's traditional Catholic views had been set out in the Statute of Six Articles and, since her religious views coincided with those of the King, the marriage brought no evident change in public policies. Anne remained a Catholic, like Henry but, because the marriage brought links with the Protestants, she has sometimes been regarded as a Protestant Queen. People identified her with Cromwell's policies and he certainly had links with some of the Lutherans. One of the charges later brought against him was that he had arranged for the King to marry 'one of his own sort'—meaning a Protestant. Her arrival was also unfairly linked with the dissolution of the monasteries which occurred at about the same time. There was an unfounded rumour that she had refused to come to England as long as 'there was still one abbey standing' and that her refusal had caused Cromwell to speed up the surrender of monastic property. Certainly, some members of her household, especially those from the continent, had close links with the Protestants. For example, Wriothesley's chronicle for May 3rd 1540 referred to three Protestants being burned at Southwark, 'for heresy against the sacrament of the altar, one was a groom of the Queen, named Maundervild, a Frenchman born.[7]

Letters in the Zurich archives show that she was generally welcomed by Protestants as Queen of England:

> The state and condition of the kingdom is much more sound and healthy since the marriage of the Queen, than it was before. She is an excellent woman and one who fears God: great hopes are entertained of a very extensive propagation of the gospel by her influence'.[8]

X Divorce

By February the King was desperately looking for a way out of the unhappy marriage. He wanted it ended quickly, hoping to escape the interminable negotiations that had attended his earlier divorce from Catherine of Aragon. He said later that he had begun remarking to Cromwell as early as February that, even though he spent nights with Anne, he had not been able to make love to her. But in spite of such comments, Henry's wish for a divorce was not made public; the French and Spanish ambassadors, who were always eager to pick up the latest court gossip, did not report it to their masters, while Cromwell, who was very well aware of Henry's wishes, referred to it later as the King's 'secret matter'. The task of finding a solution to the problem fell to Cromwell. However, he was playing a difficult dual role; Anne, understandably, looked upon him as a trusted adviser in her dealings with the King and she tried to have meetings with him to discuss her problems. But Cromwell faced a dilemma—if he was known to be giving advice to Anne, Henry would not trust him. To avoid arousing Henry's anger and suspicion, Cromwell sent secret messages to Anne telling her to try to make herself more appealing and attractive to the King who, by now, had given up hope of having any children from the marriage. Cromwell did not dare to communicate with her directly but spoke privately to her chamberlain on the King's behalf. He told the King that he had made an urgent request:

> To find some means that the Queen might be induced to order (herself) pleasantly in her behaviour towards you, thinking thereby to have some faults amended to your majesty's comfort.

Regarding the permission for the 'strange maidens' to leave, Cromwell went on to say that he had also tried to persuade them to use all pleasantness that 'she might be induced to such pleasant and honourable fashions as might have been to your Grace's comfort'.[1]

But Cromwell's intervention came too late. The King had given up hope of having children. Probably Anne had also given up hope for the marriage and no longer felt that she had any reason to make herself look attractive and amenable to Henry. After all the elaborate preparations, both in Cleves and in England, and the eager anticipation of being Queen, Henry's unexpected reaction to her must have been quite devastating. Nevertheless, she seems to have coped with it remarkably well and in a cool and rational manner. There is no direct evidence for outbursts of hysterical tears or bitter accusations against either the King or Cromwell. Perhaps because of her upbringing in Cleves, she had acquired great self-control and, while this might not be an attractive feature to Henry, it helped her to survive in England.

By learning English, she could more easily understand what was happening and gain more confidence in her own ability to deal with Henry. Certainly, he complained about her stubbornness when they were discussing some business matters concerning Princess Mary. He later described Anne's behaviour as beginning to 'wax stubborn and wilful' during Lent. Finally, he ordered Cromwell to find grounds for divorce—a bitter blow to the politician's grand ambition for an alliance between England, Cleves and the Protestant states on the continent.

Once Henry had made up his mind, things moved forward very quickly. On April 12th 1540, the published list of items of parliamentary business included the dissolution of his marriage with Anne of Cleves. On April 18th Cromwell was created Earl of Essex—probably as an incentive to arrange the divorce, with the hint of further rewards to come, if he was successful. Henry made no public show of his displeasure with Anne and he continued to treat her in a courteous, civilized manner. On the same day that Cromwell received his earldom, Henry dined with her at Westminster in the Queen's apartments. She seems to have stayed out of the public eye during most of this time, probably at Whitehall Palace. At the beginning of May, Henry and Anne appeared together in public for the last time as King and Queen. This was at a tournament in Westminster and Wriothesley described the grand occasion of jousting and feasting lasting for a week, to which many contestants were invited from France, Flanders, Scotland and Spain. It was a week of great splendour and show—even the servants of the combatants were dressed in white doublets and hose, 'cut after the Burgundian fashion'. After the jousting, the contestants went with the King and Queen to Durham Place in the Strand, the former London residence of the Bishops of Durham, where they feasted on all kinds of exotic delicacies.[2]

Although the King's immediate officials had attempted to suppress news of his 'secret matter', rumours about the failure of the marriage began to spread. Courtiers were whispering about the King's affection for Catherine Howard, 'a young lady of diminutive stature' and there was gossip that Henry was seeing her frequently during the daytime, and sometimes at midnight. Stephen Gardiner, Bishop of Winchester, actively supported this new alliance by openly providing entertainment for the couple at his palace—but people saw this as evidence of adultery, it was not yet obvious that Henry was looking for a second divorce.[3] Catherine was young, dainty, beautiful and lively—a great contrast to Anne. Henry's obsession with Catherine made him keener than ever to accomplish the divorce. As well as being young and beautiful, Catherine was backed by the powerful Howard family, headed by the Duke of Norfolk. She was about 18 years old at the time and was already a maid of honour to the Queen. Her father was Lord Edmund Howard, younger brother of the Duke of Norfolk. She had been brought up in the household of the Dowager Duchess of Norfolk and it was through the Duke's influence that she had gained her position at court. The Howards looked upon Catherine as a way of gaining further power and political advantage.

Ironically, Cromwell's own administrative reforms had thrown his enemies together. In 1539, while he was pre-eminent in the King's Privy Council, he had persuaded Parliament to pass the Act for Precedence. This act emphasized the difference between advisers who were personally appointed by the King and those who held office because of their hereditary rank. By tradition, precedence was based on ranks within the peerage; for example, a duke took precedence over a marquess, while an earl was superior to a baron in rank. Precedence further depended on the date of creation within each rank, so that the oldest title brought the highest rank. This all changed in 1539, when rank within the King's Privy Council depended on office and favour, not on heredity. This opened the way for career men, who otherwise might have been lawyers and businessmen, to become advisers to the King. They tended to be radical in their beliefs, perhaps even Protestants; they were dependent on the direct patronage of the King for their office, while they in turn used their own powers of patronage to appoint others with similar ideas. This change of status forced the so-called conservatives with Catholic leanings to act together, in opposition to Cromwell and his new men with their more radical ideas. Thomas Howard, third Duke of Norfolk, and Stephen Gardiner, Bishop of Winchester, now led the conservative element among the King's advisers. United in their opposition to Cromwell, they promoted the cause of Catherine Howard as the next Queen.[4]

In contrast to these influential figures, Anne of Cleves had no power base; she was a foreigner who had now lost her political value. She had no party in England ready to advance her cause.

The political scene in continental Europe had changed completely during the previous six months and Henry now had nothing to gain from an alliance with Cleves. On the contrary, there were signs that Charles V might be attempting to take over Gelderland by force from the Duke of Cleves. If this were to happen, England could be drawn unwillingly into an expensive war in support of Cleves. In short, the political alliance with Cleves had become an embarrassment. For less than two years Cleves had occupied a central position in European politics. It was the unreliability of his alliance with England that eventually drove William of Cleves to seek the support of the French King against Charles V.

This combination of changes in politics and the attractions of Catherine Howard persuaded Henry to move quickly towards a divorce. Anne's coronation never took place and Cromwell's great design was in ruins. His enemies at court, led by Gardiner and the Duke of Norfolk, had finally engineered his disgrace. Cromwell was arrested and sent to the Tower on trumped up charges of treason and heresy. The Act of Attainder passed against him condemned him for becoming too powerful—more powerful even than the King—and charges of heresy were based on his links with the Protestants, especially with the German Lutherans. 'The downfall of Cromwell had shown that there was no one so high, so intimate with the King, that he could be invulnerable to attack, if his faith were once suspect'.[5] Achieving a divorce for Henry was Cromwell's only hope of gaining a pardon. To add to his problems, the men who were his rivals for the King's favour took advantage of his downfall to promote the cause of Catherine Howard.

The King was clearly determined on divorce and, since he showed himself so firmly committed to it, none of his officials was likely to oppose it. However, it was important to preserve the correct legal niceties to prevent upsetting the Duke of Cleves. Anne's earlier betrothal to Francis of Lorraine cropped up once more, but it could not be seriously considered as grounds for divorce. Failure to consummate the marriage remained as the only acceptable possibility.

Although the final outcome was a foregone conclusion, it was necessary to present evidence to the church assembly of Convocation. The question of the pre-contract came up again; there was further discussion as to whether it was a contract 'de presenti' or *de futuro*. A *de presenti* betrothal involved making a contract which prohibited a later marriage with any other partner, even though there had been no 'carnal knowledge' associated with the original betrothal. A *de futuro* contract had no such force; it implied consent to a marriage at some time in the future, but it could not in any way be regarded as binding 'forever'. The certificate of annulment of the pre-contract, which the ambassadors of Cleves had promised to acquire, eventually arrived in England. However, it proved to be so vague and inconclusive that it failed to clarify the matter. It is difficult to understand the form of this document, which was described in the official records as the 'judgement signed with a berepot'. Perhaps an illustration of a beer pot was the design used on the seal of the chancery office in Cleves. Certainly the document was received in England with a certain amount of suspicion and the King's advisers found it difficult to decide whether 'the beer pot might be sufficient discharge of the former espousals'. Because the certificate was so inconclusive and could not be used as direct evidence, the only alternative was for Henry to seek a divorce based on the grounds that the marriage had not been consummated.[6]

Cromwell was eager to give his evidence in the pathetic hope of gaining a pardon. From his prison he described the King's first reactions to Anne, giving details of Henry's initial eagerness to meet her and then his utter disappointment when he saw her. He quoted the King's reluctance to marry her and then his revulsion with her after the marriage, which caused Henry to allege that she was not a virgin and that he could not bring himself to make love to her. Cromwell quoted the King's words, saying that:

> Many times his majesty has declared unto him that his nature has abhorred her ever since, so far that if his grace would (which he never mind nor thinks to do) go about to have a do with her, his highness verily thinks that his nature would not consent thereto.

Cromwell also claimed that he urged Henry to put his true feelings on paper, as proof of his lack of interest in Anne.[7]

Certainly, Henry wrote his own account of his reactions, saying that as soon as he first set eyes on Anne he considered breaking off the arrangements and that the marriage lacked his 'hearty consent'. He wrote that he had eagerly looked forward to the marriage. He had been without a wife for so long and he was 'trusting to have some assured friend, as he much doubted (distrusted) the Emperor, France and the Bishop of Rome'. He was fired with love for her since he had heard so much about 'her excellent beauty and virtuous conditions'. But his heart sank when he saw her and he lacked 'the will and the power' to consummate the marriage. He then felt glad that he had not married her without first catching sight of her, but he was sorry that she had travelled so far for the wedding. He quoted Browne and Southampton who were present at the first meeting and would corroborate his words. He also declared that his doctors, John Chamber and William Butts, together with Cromwell and the gentlemen of the Privy Chamber, would be willing to testify that he had never had any sexual relations with Anne.

Written evidence in support of the King was provided by the Lord Chancellor, the Archbishop of Canterbury, the Dukes of

Norfolk and Suffolk, the Earl of Southampton and the Bishop of Durham. They placed responsibility firmly on Cromwell, who was now in prison and awaiting execution, by saying that he had unwisely cleared, or ignored, the first obstacle to the marriage—Anne's pre-contract. Southampton said that eight days after the marriage Cromwell told him that the King had no affection for Anne and had not consummated the marriage. The others also referred to Henry's comments about his lack of interest in Anne.

Among other witnesses, Sir Thomas Heneage reported:

> Ever since the King saw the Queen, he had never liked her; and often as he went to bed with her, he mistrusted the Queen's virginity, the looseness of her breasts and other tokens; and he could have none appetite with her to do as a man should do with his wife.

Heneage went on to say that the King felt he had been badly served by the men that he had trusted. Sir Anthony Denny made a similar deposition, saying that the King had complained to him about her slack breasts and about her suspect virginity which made him unable to love her. Denny also quoted the King's words, presenting Henry's lament that poor men were happier than princes because they could choose their wives for themselves. Sir Thomas Wriothesley, one of the King's secretaries, quoted a conversation that he had with Cromwell, in which Cromwell referred to the King's 'great matter' of Henry's dislike of Anne. Wriothesley realistically went on to urge Cromwell to devise a way out for the King 'for if he remained in this grief and trouble, they would all one day smart for it'.

Both of Henry's doctors supported the views of the courtiers and declared that the marriage had not been consummated. Dr Chamber reported that, on the morning after the wedding night, the King told him that he had no sexual relations with the Queen. This had happened on several other occasions as well and Henry had asked him for his advice. At which the doctor told him 'not to enforce himself' because weakness would result and his health would suffer. Chamber went on to say that the King found her body 'so disordered and indisposed to excite him and provoke any lust in him, that his majesty could not be provoked or stirred to that act'. Dr Butts made the same kind of reports. He said that the

King had told him of his failure to consummate the marriage, but because he continued to produce two 'nightly emissions' in his sleep, he felt he was still capable of sexual relations, but not with Anne. The Queen's ladies reported that she had told them that she was not pregnant and that no consummation had ever occurred. All this so-called 'evidence' was presented as a more powerful argument than the dubious validity of the 'judgement of the beer pot'.

The legal procedures advanced with great speed. On July 7th 1540 the archbishops, bishops and other members of Convocation met in the chapter house at Westminster. Richard Gwent, an official of Convocation, presented the King's letters of commission, addressed to the archbishops and clergy, which were read to the assembled company. Following Gwent's presentation, the clergy agreed to proceed with the commission. The Bishop of Winchester, Stephen Gardiner, went on to explain the grounds for annulling the marriage. After his explanation, a committee was formed, consisting of the Archbishops of Canterbury and York, the Bishops of London, Durham, Winchester and Worcester, and eight officials of Convocation who would then examine the evidence in detail and explain it to a full meeting of Convocation. The committee agreed that the Bishops of Durham and Winchester, with a few other leading clergymen, should examine the evidence of witnesses and report to Convocation the following day.

The same afternoon, between 1 pm and 6 pm, at Westminster, the members of the committee had discussions with the Lord Chancellor, the Dukes of Norfolk and Suffolk, the Earl of Southampton, various members of the King's Privy Chamber and Dr Butts. Dr Chamber was interviewed separately in his house at Cannon Row. They were all questioned about the validity of the written evidence they had submitted earlier. On the following day (July 8th) four lawyers joined the committee and the members held further discussions about the King's commission. At 3 pm the Archbishop of Canterbury called a full meeting of Convocation at which it was agreed that the King and Queen were no longer bound by their marriage. The committee of twelve clergy and lawyers were made responsible for drawing up official documents of annulment for the King, to be presented to Convocation the next day.

At 3 pm on July 9th, the letters testimonial, containing the judgement of annulment were presented to the assembly, written on parchment and signed by the officials. The letters stated that because of doubts and perplexities and, after mature deliberation, the clergy had found that the marriage was null. They based their decision on Anne's pre-contract, which made the marriage of dubious legality, and went on to state that it was entered into unwillingly and was never consummated. It was a procedure which later led Gilbert Burnet, Bishop of Salisbury (1643-1715) to describe their decision as 'the greatest piece of compliance that ever the King had from the clergy'. As a result of the judgement, both the King and Queen were free to marry whoever they wished. A parliamentary statute cynically gave the official version:

> We consider your majesty not be bound by the pretensed marriage, which is of itself nought and of no force, so your majesty, without tarrying for any judgement may—contract and consummate matrimony with any other woman. The Lady Anne did of her own free will assent and has openly confessed that she remains not carnally known of the King's body. She has also signified her confession by a letter subscribed in her own hand. And the Lady Anne shall not be named or called the King's wife.

Following the judgement, the penalty of high treason was imposed on anyone who might dispute the decision. But to remove the anxieties of those who had helped to bring about the divorce, they were pardoned for any actions which might have been interpreted as treasonable. However, any such pardon did not apply to Cromwell, who was awaiting execution. In fact, the pre-contract itself had not been binding on Anne, but it was used as a pretext to give Henry what he wanted—divorce from Anne, disentanglement from the Cleves alliance, and freedom to marry Catherine Howard.[8]

Perhaps to prevent large numbers of people taking advantage of the new legislation to obtain similar divorces on the grounds of a pre-contract, a further statute was quickly issued. It declared that, from July 1st onwards, marriages which had been carried out in the Church of England and then consummated, were indissoluble, in spite of any unconsummated pre-contract.[9]

XI   Settlement

As soon as Convocation had pronounced the divorce on July 10th, the next stage was to arrange a settlement that would be acceptable to all parties, including the Duke of Cleves. While all these legal negotiations were taking place in London, Anne and her household were staying at Richmond Palace. This was just a few miles out of London, where she had been sent on the pretext of avoiding an outbreak of the plague. It was very important for Henry and his advisers to gain her co-operation, if the divorce was to proceed smoothly and quickly.

On July 6th, before Convocation had met, Henry's ministers had already visited Anne at Richmond and, through an interpreter, they had the difficult task of explaining to her about the divorce. Rutland, who was Anne's chamberlain at the time, wrote of her reaction. He said that she took the matter 'heavily', but he tried to comfort her by explaining that the King would deal fairly with her and that the outcome would depend on the decision of the clergy—for this reason, she had no need to be fearful. Rutland described the events to Cromwell:

> At 4 o'clock this morning the Duke of Cleves' ambassador came to the Queen. She called us to her chamber and declared by the ambassador that the King had sent a message which required an answer. I did see her to take the matter heavily, I desired her to be of good comfort and that the King's highness is so gracious and virtuous a Prince that he would (do) nothing but that should stand with the law of God to upset his conscience and hers, the peace of the realm and lords and commons.

Anne listened to his explanations and said nothing. The unspoken threat of execution must have had a powerful effect. Her self-control was truly remarkable—Henry's officials reported that she heard the news 'without alteration of countenance' and agreed to comply with the King's wishes, but she stubbornly refused to provide a written agreement. However, they felt confident from her reactions that, in time, she would co-operate fully and they believed that the King's commission could be successfully presented to Convocation on the following day. By ostensibly leaving the divorce to the decision of the clergy, Henry distanced himself from direct involvement in it. This also allowed Anne to have the face-saving device of accepting the divorce as a decision of churchmen, rather than outright rejection by Henry.

Once Anne had made a verbal acceptance of the divorce, it was necessary for the King to have her agreement in writing to avoid future recriminations and especially objections from her brother. On July 11th, in the Queen's inner chamber at Richmond, Anne signed letters to the King, acknowledging her full acceptance of the divorce. She signed herself 'your majesty's most humble sister and servant, Anne, daughter of Cleves', deliberately writing the word 'sister' as a sign of her future status. However, these letters were not enough. She was required to go further and write to her brother in German, as clear evidence that she was fully aware of what was happening. This was a move to deter the Duke from seeking the help of Charles V or Francis I in an alliance against England. Anne was also assured that she would be safe in England, even if William joined such an alliance.

On July 12th Suffolk, Southampton and Wriothesley saw Anne again at Richmond. They presented her with the divorce settlement; this was a deliberately generous arrangement which formally gave her the status of the King's sister, provided she accepted the terms of the agreement. Henry wrote 'continuing your conformity, you shall find us a perfect friend, content to repute you as our dearest sister'. Her allowance included £4000 a year in revenues, two houses, Richmond Palace and Bletchingley in Surrey (which lies about 17 miles to the south of London) with their splendid houses and parks, and an annual income of £500. In addition, the settlement allowed her to keep all her hangings and plate; there was money for the upkeep of her household, and she could retain her dresses, jewels and pearls. Henry's ministers sent him an account of the meeting. They reported that they went to her chamber and gave her the documents together with the King's token present of 500 marks. She then left the room to discuss the terms with her interpreter. After a while, she returned and demanded to know where Bletchingley was, probably thinking that she was being banished to some distant and remote corner of the country. She then asked further questions about her status and her future household. She was clearly unwilling to write to her brother, saying 'Why should I write to my brother before he write to me? It were not meet'. In her view, if she wrote first, William would be anxious about her and would assume that she was in danger and in need of help. But she agreed that the King should see any letters that came from her brother.

Anne wrote to Henry from Richmond on July 16th thanking him for his 'goodness, favour and liberality' and assuring him that she had not changed her mind and was content with her settlement. Her letters reveal her determination to keep to the agreement and she indicated her resolve,

> which is correspondent and agreeable to my first mind and answer made at the first opening of this matter unto me, from the which, as I neither have varied from the beginning, nor will vary hereafter, so, if any man have said the contrary, I assure your Grace that he hath done it without my consent or commission.

However, she did change her mind about writing to her brother. Henry was insistent that she wrote to William and understood what she was writing. He refused to accept the uncertainty of her verbal promise—'all will remain uncertain upon a woman's promise'. Henry's officials finally persuaded her and gained what they wanted and, just over a week later, she wrote to Cleves after William had written to Henry expressing disapproval of the divorce. She clearly found it a very difficult letter to write—she had to admit to her brother that the marriage was finished.

Anne wrote to him saying she preferred him to know the truth from her and that she had no complaints, 'I account god pleased with what is done and know myself to have suffered no wrong injury, but being my body preserved with the integrity which I brought in to this realm'. She characteristically added the words—'and being the matter thus finished'. She went on to say that she would be treated by Henry in a fatherly and brotherly fashion. 'I find the King's highness, whom I cannot have justly as my husband, to be nevertheless, as a most kind, loving and friendly father and brother'. She considered that she was contented and satisfied and she anxiously urged William to take no action on her behalf. In her letter she stated that she was willing to accept the decision of the clergy over the divorce. She clearly wanted her brother to understand that she truly accepted the situation and wrote that when 'the nobles and commons of this realm desired the King's highness to commit the examination of the matter of marriage between his Majesty and me, to the examination and determination of the whole Clergy of this realm, I did willingly consent thereunto'. She then went on to say that 'out of her respect for the truth' she had agreed that the marriage had not been consummated.

Her choice of the words 'sister', 'father' and 'brother' are significant; they show her relationship to Henry, in which he was depicted as her male protector and provider, taking on the roles of her father and brother, rather than husband and lover. She also gave her brother full details of the settlement, saying that she had the status of the King's sister, she was being generously treated and intended to stay in England. In addition, she wished her mother to know that she was completely satisfied with the arrangements. While this letter was a deliberate attempt by the King and his ministers to deflect the Duke's resentment, Anne was similarly anxious to dissuade her brother from taking reckless action on her behalf, which might cause endless political problems for her homeland. When she discovered that a nephew of Olisleger was carrying the letters to Cleves, she asked to meet him and she gave him a personal message for her brother to report that she was happy and was being well-treated. After she had dined that evening, she returned her wedding ring to Henry, calmly desiring 'that it might be broken in pieces, as a thing which she knew of no force or value'.

On July 24th she received a letter from her brother which she sent to the King, who read it and returned it to her. On July 28th Cromwell was executed, having played his part in securing the divorce. On that same day, Henry married Catherine Howard at

Oatlands in Surrey, at the new palace that he had begun to build in 1538.

The speed with which this divorce and remarriage were carried out was in total contrast to the events leading up to the divorce from Catherine of Aragon and Henry's subsequent marriage to Anne Boleyn. Henry had clearly learned from his previous experience and did not want a similar situation to arise. Catherine's last pregnancy had occurred in 1518 and it was obvious that, by the age of 40 and after so many unsuccessful pregnancies, she was unlikely to produce a male heir. However, this did not directly affect her status and, although Henry was no longer her lover, she was still his wife and Queen of England. In spite of all the problems that she had endured, she dearly loved the King and for nine years she maintained her belief in him and in their marriage. Shakespeare, in his play *Henry VIII*, gives a sense of the nobility of her character, when he describes her as 'although unqueened, yet like a queen'. (*Henry VIII*, act 2, scene 2).

Catherine had regarded Henry's chief minister, Wolsey, as the cause of her ills. She felt that she was a victim of his ambitious political programme to link England with France rather than with the Spanish empire, whose representative was the Emperor, Charles V, her uncle. In his attempt to dissolve the marriage and break the links with Spain, Wolsey brought up the pretext of the former betrothal between Catherine and Henry's deceased elder brother, Prince Arthur. In this we can see the similarities with Anne of Cleves—a former contract which had been annulled was produced as evidence for divorce. In the case of Catherine and Arthur, the pre-contract had been thoroughly investigated before her marriage to Henry. The Pope had provided a legal dispensation for the pre-contract and the marriage that followed was formally approved. However, after a marriage lasting 18 years which had failed to produce a male heir, Catherine's former betrothal to Arthur suddenly became a pretext for divorce. As Shakespeare succinctly put it:

Lord Chamberlain: It seems the marriage with his brother's wife has crept too near his conscience.

Suffolk: No, his conscience has crept too near another lady.[1]

Catherine herself had no doubts about the validity of her marriage to Henry—she had never married his elder brother and there had been no question of any consummation of the proposed marriage with Arthur.

Henry assumed the attitude that, because his wife had not produced an heir, they had incurred the disapproval of God—suggesting that either the Pope's dispensation was at fault or that the Pope himself did not have the power to make such a dispensation. Henry had various love affairs while he was married to Catherine and had fathered an illegitimate son, known as the Duke of Richmond but, as far as Catherine was concerned, she was still his wife. When ideas of divorce began to circulate, she had no intention of giving up her position and appealed to her uncle, Charles V, for help. However, like Anne of Cleves in the same situation, when she saw that there was a risk of blood being shed on her behalf, with the prospect of an invasion by Spain, she eventually agreed to the divorce nine years after it was first proposed. In spite of her consistent opposition, she was finally forced to accept that the pre-contract with Arthur had invalidated her marriage to his brother Henry.

Having endured such protracted negotiations, wrangles and arguments to obtain his first divorce, Henry was determined to avoid such a repetition with his second divorce. He achieved his aim with the aid of Anne's ready compliance and the summary arrest of Cromwell, who was pathetically keen to prosecute the divorce in the hope of escaping execution.

As soon as the divorce was announced Anne, who had been queen for just over six months, became the Lady Anne of Cleves. Like Catherine of Aragon, she was now 'a queen unqueened'. From the time of the divorce, she signed her letters 'Anna, Daughter of Cleves'. In official documents she was described as 'Anna, Daughter of the late Duke of Cleves, Julich, Gelderland and Bar' (this latter duchy lay to the south of Cleves) and 'sister of William, Duke of Cleves etc.' Just a few reminders of Anne's short reign still exist. The chapel royal at St James's Palace, Westminster, was completed in 1540 and the painted compartments of the ceiling contain heraldic designs, mottoes and monograms of Anne and Henry. The letters H and A, with the date 1540, stand out clearly. The decoration also contains the names of the four German states of Berg, Cleves, Julich and Mark, which made up the duchy of Cleves. Secondly, the headboard of a royal bed forms part of the Burrell Collection in Glasgow—it bears the date 1539 and the initials H and A. Made of painted oak, it shows carved figures on each side, one male and one female, dressed in armour. Perhaps as symbols of Henry's hopes and desires for the marriage, a lewd cherub hovers over the male figure and a pregnant cherub stands above the female figure.[1]

Apart from the Earl of Rutland's comment that he comforted her at Richmond when she first received the news about the divorce, we know very little about Anne's reactions or emotions. In spite of the divorce, she seems to have remained fond of Henry or, at any rate, she kept any feelings of hostility well hidden. When Henry wrote to two members of his household, Edward Carne, who had gone to Cleves as one of the negotiators of the marriage, and Sir John Wallop, he described her state of mind at the news of the divorce. He said that he had first obtained her consent to leave the matter to the clergy and, when she learned of the decision, 'she was troubled and perplexed, in consequence of the great love and affection which she seemed to have only to our person'. Out of this great love for him, she consented to the divorce.

There are just a few clues about her personality—Henry had already complained about her stubbornness and it is clear that it took more than a week for the King's advisers to persuade her to write to her brother outlining the reasons for the divorce. Perhaps it was her strong will and determination that carried her through the difficult period from January to June 1540. She must have found it unnerving to be Queen in a foreign court, surrounded by intrigue and gossip, in a country whose laws, customs and language were totally unknown to her. Before her she always had the examples of the long-drawn out divorce of Catherine of Aragon and the execution of Anne Boleyn. She really had no choice. If she had taken any action to oppose the divorce, she must have been fully aware that she risked execution and that her brother might have felt obliged to take action to avenge the insult to his sister—a process which was very likely to bring disaster to Cleves. In the event, William lacked the resources to act and he commented realistically that he was glad she had fared no worse. By admitting that the marriage was not consummated, whether it was true or not, she saved herself from death and both her brother and her country from danger. Her reactions suggest that she had an intelligent, practical attitude to life. Only she and Henry really knew the truth and, by complying with Henry's wishes, Anne gained independence, position and security.

Marillac gave his opinion, saying that she wished to please Henry and stay in this country. However, he also said that the King had forbidden vicars and ministers to visit her—an action which upset the people whose love she had gained. They esteemed her as one of the most sweet, gracious and humane royal wives they had known and they greatly desired her to continue with them as their Queen. Marillac went on to say 'the King is going to marry a young lady of extraordinary beauty—the Queen takes it all in good part'.[2]

The most immediate and obvious difference to her life was in the size and status of her household. Her household was already somewhat depleted since some of the women who originally came with her from Cleves had already returned before the divorce. After the divorce, she was no longer surrounded by ambitious English noble lords and ladies. There was very little prospect of advancement and political gain in the court of an ex-queen. As a result of her changed circumstances, the number of her officials and attendants fell from about 130 to a more modest 30. Her chief officials were her chamberlain Sir William Goring, her steward Jasper Horsey, and Wymond Carew, her receiver, who also acted as an interpreter. Lady Lisle eventually achieved her ambition of having her daughter, Katherine Basset, as an attendant to Anne of Cleves, but only after the divorce, when she was just Lady Anne and not the Queen of England. Anne also had two other English officials, while the rest were from Cleves. Among these were seven gentlemen, her physician, Dr Cornelius Cepher, two 'dutchwomen' named Katherine and Gertrude, Mathyew her secretary, Schoulenberg the cook, Henry the butler, and five other male servants. Their total wages came to about £500 a year. However, they may not have been totally dependant on Anne for their income. For example, her cup-bearer, Warner van Gymnych, was dealing in beer—he obtained a licence to export nearly 20,000 gallons of it. From choice, she seems to have created for herself a model of the court at Cleves, surrounding herself with friends and compatriots who shared her interests.

On her marriage, she had received an equivalent amount of property to Jane Seymour. After the divorce, she was no longer entitled to such a large allowance but she received large amounts of property, on condition that she stayed in England. If she returned to Cleves, she would lose much of her income. In a strange turn of fate, she received a great deal of property which suddenly became available from the forfeited estates of Cromwell. He had taken advantage of the dissolution of the monasteries to acquire large amounts of monastic property, much of it lying in Essex and Sussex. In this way she acquired many of the properties in Sussex that had belonged to the priories of Lewes and Michelham before the dissolution. These were readily available for Anne, together with further manors in Leicestershire, Northampton-shire, Oxfordshire, Surrey and Yorkshire, all of which had once belonged to Cromwell. She acquired other property that had once belonged to Sir Nicholas Carew, who had been executed for treason in 1539. This had been in the hands of the King since Carew's execution and was immediately available for the grant. Bletchingley, with its splendid house and two deer parks, was formerly held by Carew. In addition to the lands of Carew and Cromwell, she received many manors in Suffolk, including some which had previously belonged to Charles Brandon, Duke of Suffolk. Another substantial amount of property came to Anne from Bisham Abbey in Berkshire, now also dissolved. Nearer to London, she received grants of three manors in Kent: Hever, Kemsing and Seal. Of these, Hever boasted a castle and an extensive park. The castle was a moated, semi-fortified house dating from the fourteenth and fifteenth centuries. Since 1462 it had been the home of the Boleyns—the family which had produced Anne Boleyn. Anne's father, Sir Thomas Boleyn, had died in 1538 and the King had taken over the house. Consequently, it was available to be granted to Anne of Cleves in 1540. Rents from these generous grants of property were intended to provide her with a substantial income of about £4000 a year.[1]

In addition to Cromwell's lands, she also received some of the contents of his houses and, in August 1540, the royal officials were busy moving 'furniture' out of Cromwell's houses in London 'for the use of the Lady Anne'.

By August there were already minor quarrels within her modest household, principally centred around her receiver, Wymond Carew. He had previously been in the employ of Jane Seymour, being responsible for the income from her lands. When her property passed to Anne, he continued to act as administrator for the same lands. After the divorce, he remained in Anne's service, but he was not content with his status. He wrote to John Gate of the King's Privy Chamber, requesting an increase in his wages. He and his wife received a wage of £20 a year, while the steward Horsey and his wife received £26 13s 4d, which caused a certain amount of ill-feeling between the two families. The trouble was probably caused by Carew's wife, who felt that she was unfairly esteemed at 'two degrees below' Mrs Horsey. If he and his wife did not receive the increase which they requested, Carew asked to be moved from the household because Anne was particularly displeased with him, having discovered that he was intercepting her letters. In fact, he had been appointed by the Duke of Suffolk to inform the King and his advisers about any letters that she received. Carew had obediently carried out his spying activities and reported to the Privy Chamber that she had received letters from her brother, which she did not intend to show to Henry. When Carew made further enquiries, he found that they were merely letters 'of congratulation' from her brother. Nevertheless, he suggested that it was in the interests of Anne's own security to ensure that the King should see them. Although Anne distrusted him and he disliked his office, he stayed on in her household for several more years and he acted as her agent and go-between in dealing with the King.

In spite of such minor difficulties in her household, Anne seems to have welcomed the independence of her new life. Once she gained control over her life, she seems to have relaxed and enjoyed herself. The French ambassador wrote in August that Henry had visited her at Richmond in August and he seemed so happy there that some people were suggesting that he might re-marry her. However, Marillac, on a more realistic note, added that Henry brought his legal advisers with him and was, in fact, making sure that she would not cause any difficulties in the future. Marillac also commented on Anne's obvious happiness—'Madame la Cleve, far from pretending to be married, is as joyous as ever and wears new dresses every day, which argues either prudent dissimulation or stupid forgetfulness'. In September he wrote 'Madame of Cleves has a more joyous countenance than ever. She wears a great variety of dresses, and passes all her time in sports and recreations'.[2]

In his earlier years, Henry VIII had been a keen sportsman, playing active games like tennis and bowls, while he gambled extensively on cards, dice and dominoes. Anne seems to have taken up such pastimes with enthusiasm and she had plenty of opportunity to indulge in all forms of sport and recreation at Richmond. An innovative feature of Henry VII's design for the palace was the gardens, which had wooden galleries at first floor level. From these, viewers could see the gardens from above. This was the best way of admiring the intricate knot patterns and complicated layout of Tudor gardens. At the lower end of the gardens there were other galleries or 'houses of pleasure', designed for games like chess, dice and cards, and there were archery butts, bowling alleys and places for playing tennis.[3] All this was further enhanced by a magnificent deer park. Henry VIII did not seem particularly attached to the palace at Richmond and had granted it to Wolsey when Wolsey presented him with the gift of Hampton Court. In 1530, following Wolsey's fall, the palace had returned to the King's hands and so, like Bletchingley, it was available to be given to Anne in 1540. In addition to the facilities for sport and entertainment, Anne had the use of the great hall, chapel and library, as well as the extensive private apartments.[4]

XIV   A New Role

We have already seen that Carew was acting as an informer within her household to alert the King and his counsellors of any political manoeuvres on her behalf. Anne herself deliberately kept well away from politics—but the surveillance continued. For example, letters to her from Calais were intercepted in 1541. In the event, they were found to be written not to Anne, but to Mrs Howard, 'the old Duchess of Norfolk's woman', to Mrs Sympson and Katherine Bassett, daughter of Lady Lisle, who were both women of Anne's household. Although these letters proved to be unimportant, they show how Anne's contacts were kept under constant surveillance because there was always a chance that she might become a threat in the future and a focus of discontent. However, she was always very careful to keep out of danger by distancing herself from any political intrigue.

While Henry continued to visit Anne at Richmond from time to time, she was also welcomed at court. The Spanish ambassador, Chapuys, wrote in January 1541 that Anne of Cleves seemed happier than ever and that, since Queen Catherine was not yet pregnant, people were beginning to spread gossip that Henry might become reconciled with Anne. Chapuys also described her New Year gift to the King—two fine large horses, caparisoned in mauve velvet, with trappings to match. This forms a strange contrast with Henry's New Year present of sable furs to her at the first meeting in January 1540, which he could not face giving her in person. Early in January 1541 Anne was staying at Hampton Court with the rest of the court. On her arrival, she had been received by the Duchess of Suffolk and the Countess of Dartford, who had both been part of her former royal household. Anne seems to have had a particular friendship with the Duchess of Suffolk, who had welcomed her on her first arrival in England. After greeting her, the ladies then took Anne for a formal meeting with Queen Catherine.

This could have been a very difficult situation for both women. Chapuys says that Anne had to wait while Catherine took advice from the chancellor, Audley, and the Earl of Sussex about how she should greet her predecessor. Anne then entered the room

> as if she herself were the most insignificant damsel about Court, all the time addressing the Queen on her knees, notwithstanding the prayers and entreaties of the latter, who received her most kindly, showing her great favour and courtesy.

In acting like this, Anne deliberately made a great effort to stress her own unimportance and insignificance and so avoided any hint of competition and rivalry with Catherine. With her unassuming temperament and distance from politics, she posed no obvious threat to the new Queen of England.

After the two women had met, Henry himself came in and bowed to Anne and embraced and kissed her. At supper he and Catherine sat in their usual places, while Anne sat near the bottom of the table, apparently looking cheerful and unconcerned. After supper, the three of them conversed and when Henry retired early for the night, the two women danced together. We have seen that music and dancing had not been acceptable at Cleves as suitable pastimes for noble ladies, but Anne must have quickly learned the ways of the English court. The same procedures were repeated the next day and the three were happily engaged in 'conversation, amusement and mirth'. Henry gave Catherine a gift of a ring and two small dogs, which the Queen then passed on to Anne, whether as her own gift, or on Henry's behalf, it is impossible to know. After dinner on the second day, Anne rode back to Richmond. Through her own good sense, strength of character and adaptability, she had coped with an extremely difficult and delicate situation.[1]

Marillac had been puzzled by Anne's reactions. He could not decide whether she was clever enough to conceal her true feelings or whether she was too stupid to understand what was happening to her. However, the way in which she prepared herself for her encounter with Catherine indicates a good deal of intelligent planning and forethought. By deliberately presenting herself as a person of no importance, she allowed the Queen to take the initiative and receive her with royal graciousness. This was a tactful and courteous way of gaining Catherine's confidence. The comment that the two women danced together after Henry had gone to bed suggests that they were able to share some kind of rapport. This particular episode is significant since it shows that, after spending a year in England, Anne could now converse easily in English and had also learned to dance.

XV Domestic Life

Anne spent a great deal of her time at Richmond. Very little of the palace now remains, but it was one of the first great Tudor palaces, built originally for Henry VII. The lavish royal apartments were set in the privacy of a great stone keep which had been built in the medieval style, while the gardens and lodgings were linked with timber galleries. It was a place where she had plenty of opportunity to take part in the sport and recreation that she obviously enjoyed.[1] She retained the house until 1547 and, while she may have been responsible for repairs during that time, she seems to have spent very little money on it, probably finding more agreeable uses for her income.[2] Although Anne clearly made use of the amenities of Richmond Palace, she also spent time at her other main house in Bletchingley, which was more of a comfortable country house than a royal palace. In 1540, Thomas Cawarden was made keeper of the house and parks at Bletchingley and held the role of Anne's steward there. As keeper and steward, he had lodgings within the main house, together with a separate house for his own use within the park.

Cawarden was a close associate of the King, being a member of his Privy Chamber and also the keeper of Henry's wonderful new palace of Nonsuch in Surrey, which the King began to build in 1538 in celebration of the birth of Prince Edward. Rather like Cromwell, Cawarden was a 'new man'—a man of humble origins, whose personality, energy and undoubted abilities of organization attracted the attention of the King. By 1544, he was holding the official title of master of tents and revels to the King with a salary of £40 a year. In this position, he was in charge of the royal 'pavilions, hales, tents, revels and masques'. His duties involved storing and checking a large collection of stage properties and organizing new properties for court entertainments. He paid the tailors and carpenters and ordered new materials. He was also responsible for the design and upkeep of very elaborate silk-hung tents and canopies, many of them decked with cloth of gold and silver similar to those seen in the painting of the Field of Cloth of Gold which shows Henry's meeting with Francis I in 1520. Cawarden held the position of a theatrical manager during the mid-sixteenth century—in the period before the plays of William Shakespeare were performed. He may have supplied the equipment for plays such as Nicholas Udall's *Roister Doister* and William Stevenson's *Gammer Gurton's Needle*—both of them riotously entertaining comedies. This was the time when private theatres were setting the trends which were later taken up by the public theatres.

However, tents were not only used for entertainments, they were also an essential part of military equipment. In his capacity as master of tents, Cawarden accompanied the King on campaign in France in 1544. As a result of his administrative abilities, he was rewarded with a knighthood, conferred on him 'at the King's lodgings at Boulogne'. Because Cawarden was so high in Henry's favour, he was allowed to keep a company of 40 armed and liveried retainers, as well as a large number of domestic and official servants. Also because of his royal connections, Cawarden was in a position to employ distinguished Italian artists to decorate his house at Blackfriars in London, which lay on the site of the former religious house of Blackfriars.[3]

Anne stayed at Bletchingley from time to time in the house that had been largely rebuilt in about 1500 for Edward Stafford, the third Duke of Buckingham. Set on and around the site of a medieval manor-house, it had been made into an extensive Tudor country house of about 63 rooms on at least two floors, with the added amenity of two large, well-stocked deer parks. When Buckingham was executed for treason in 1521 it had passed to Sir Nicholas Carew and was again vacant and available to Anne in 1540 after Carew had been executed for treason in 1539. We know that she and her household spent time at Bletchingley, since the parish registers there have recorded the deaths of some of Anne's staff, including her physician, Dr Cepher, and her chaplain, Mathew Lother. The churchwardens' accounts note that she once borrowed a *sanctus* bell from the church and failed to return it. She also wrote letters from Bletchingley, including one to Princess Mary. Perhaps she enjoyed the hunting in the parks—certainly, in

Anne of Cleves. The portrait has been attributed to the workshop of Barthel Bruyn (1493-1555).

Thomas Cromwell was created Earl of Essex in 1540. He was the King's chief minister 1533-40.

Anne of Cleves. This portrait has also been attributed to the workshop of Barthel Bruyn. X-ray photography has revealed the inscription 'Anne, by grace of God Queen of England, daughter of John, third Duke (of Cleves)' above her right shoulder.

Henry VIII painted by an unknown artist, c. 1542.

Mary Tudor at the age of 28, painted by Master John.

Bletchingley, Surrey. The gatehouse is a visible remnant of the former large Tudor country-house.

Hever Castle, Kent. Anne received Hever Castle in 1540 as part of the divorce settlement.

Penshurst Place, Kent. Anne gave up Bletchingley and received Penshurst Place in exchange.

1543 Albert, Duke of Prussia, mentioned that he had sent her a gift of a hawk. He sent 12 falcons to the King and enquired whether 'Henry's queen, of the line of the Duke of Juliers', had received the hawk which he had sent to her the previous year. In 1546 she leased the house, the parks and the manor of Bletchingley to Cawarden but she continued to reside there at times, while Cawarden and his wife Elizabeth probably lived nearby at Hextalls, in the large double-courtyard keeper's house within the North Park.[4]

An inventory of the main house in 1559 gives us some idea of the status of the contents. Although it was compiled immediately after the death of Cawarden and two years after Anne had died, some of the remaining contents may have been Anne's. When they were compiling the inventory, the valuers completed a circuit of the upstairs rooms first, beginning with the upper gallery. This gallery, or corridor, provided access to individual rooms without passing through any of the others—an indication of the increasing value placed on privacy during Tudor times. The gallery gave access to the great chamber, which was the state bedchamber, furnished with a walnut four-poster bed and walnut furniture. Furniture of walnut wood was highly prized; for example, Henry had ordered a great bed of 'walnutree' in 1530 for his new palace at Westminster. While the construction material might be expensive, the curtains and hangings were likely to be even more costly, especially when they consisted of cloth of gold and silver. At Bletchingley, as well as bed curtains of cloth of gold and silver, there were cushions of similar materials, some combined with coloured silks. The walls of the great chamber were covered with about forty yards of tapestry, giving some indication of the size of the room. A small lobby led to another bedroom which was described as the 'chamber over the parlour'. This was another large room, with a further forty yards of tapestry around the walls and another tapestry over the fireplace. Reference to a long window-cushion suggests that there was a window seat, perhaps in a south-facing bay window overlooking the courtyard. The bedchamber at the top of the stairs was another well-furnished room, with contents similar to those of the great chamber. This room was in an important position at the top of the stairs, with the staircase providing an impressive approach to it. Both the great chamber and the chamber at the top of the stairs had smaller bedrooms adjoining them, as rooms for members of the household.

Most of the rooms on the upper floor had curtains and cushions of silk and satin in a variety of colours, ranging from yellow and blue to red and green. The main rooms on the ground floor—the hall and two parlours—were for public use, and contained long trestle tables for dining. There is also evidence for leisure pursuits, as these rooms and the lobbies between them contained several gaming tables and musical intruments.

The buttery, cellar and spicery formed the next set of rooms and lay close to the hall. Other rooms provided lodgings for staff on the first floor, while the service rooms were on the ground floor. These included a starching-house (for starching linen), a milking house, a bake-house, a brew-house and a mill-house containing a horse-powered malt mill. There was also a well-equipped kitchen. However, the large armoury, which was described in the inventory of 1559, was clearly the property of Cawarden who played a major role in organizing rebellion against the Catholic regime of Queen Mary in the years 1554-6.

Most of the house had been demolished by 1680 and only the centre brick-built gate-house now stands above ground. During the sixteenth century, the same gate-house was crowned with a tower containing a bell 'to call the folks to meals'. Excavations of part of the house, including a large cellar for wine and beer, have revealed decorated floor tiles, pottery and stoneware vessels from the continent, which date from the mid-sixteenth century. Other features still remaining include contemporary garderobes and drains.

Cawarden took his responsibilities as keeper and steward of Bletchingley very seriously, which led to a certain amount of friction between him and Anne about the management of the house and parks. He complained bitterly of her stubborn refusal to spend money on repairing the house and he accused her of putting up unnecessary buildings—a brewhouse and an inn. He criticized her staff for cutting down good timber trees for firewood and then wasting the timber. He went on to complain of Anne's unwillingness to apologize to the park-keeper's wife for causing so much trouble concerning the trees. In an undated document he described his grievances at her behaviour as follows:

> I gave her Grace wood for dispendinge in the house sythen (since) her first comynge thether, of greate Oke, beache and Asshe by fowere, five, syx and seven score lodes at a tyme.

> And at hallowtyde laste, I gave them at there requeste ageanste her Graces comynge thether, syx hundred lode of wood or there aboutes by there owne reporte, which before the havinge thereof, theye sought by waye of requeste.

> After I had gyven them the seide lodes of wood, they seide it was there owne and that they myghte by present patente take it where and when they wolde and that I myght nor oughte not denye them.

> And in myne absens her Officers did commence the making of coles and felled doune myne woodes by the grounde for the same, also fayre Okes, Asshes and Beches beinge good tymber wood (Which they never presumed nor the lyke before this tyme) made to the number of 40 lodes and also besydes A greate deale which yet remanithe uncoled.

> Also where I did appoynte and delyver at her requeste sufficiente tymber for the necessarie reparinge of the house, they without myne (con)sente and Knoleage did fell A greate meanye of tymber trees and thereof made fower newe houses of tymber and borde where none (was) before, which cannot be justified by the lawe.

> Also with my seide wooddes did furnesshe A commune Bruhouse and also a vittelynge house in the contreye not without A greate nomber of Lodes and that of no (worse) wood than is before resyted (recited).

At the urgent request of Sir William Goring of the royal household, who was also Anne's chamberlain and was attempting to keep the peace between the two sides, Cawarden provided Anne with the 40 loads of charcoal that her staff requested. However,

Cawarden tried to stipulate that she should make an official acknowledgement that she had received the charcoal as a gift from him. In addition, he wanted her to offer the park-keeper's wife an apron, by way of recompense for the trouble she had caused. In spite of various attempts at conciliation, the friction continued; Cawarden failed to gain any satisfaction and he made further complaints that she refused to offer the apron to the park-keeper's wife, as he requested, and that her staff continued to destroy the valuable timber trees. Even the envoy from Cleves was drawn into the dispute. In 1551 he approached the Privy Council and persuaded the Privy Councillors to allow Anne to have full, official access to the house at Bletchingley. With such access, she was granted the use 'of the woods there for fire, doing no waste or spoil'.

In reply to Cawarden's criticisms, Anne complained about him, because he was late in paying his rent for Bletchingley. On December 11th 1554 she wrote to him from Hever Castle in Kent saying that she had already been waiting there for a week for his payment, which by then was nearly three months overdue. She was anxious to have the money before travelling to Penshurst where she intended to spend Christmas—'for I have a fair home and would fane be going before the holyday'. Although there was clearly a great deal of aggravation between two strong and contrasting personalities, Cawarden remained as her steward until her death.

We have seen that Wymond Carew had been her receiver until 1543, when he transferred to become receiver to Henry's sixth wife, Catherine Parr. After Wymond had left Anne's household, Thomas Carew, another member of the same family, took up the post of her receiver and he handled the correspondence between Anne and Cawarden.

Anne's letters provide evidence that she stayed at Hever Castle, the former home of the Boleyns, which lies between Bletchingley and Penshurst. As well as writing to Cawarden from Hever, she also wrote to Queen Mary in 1554, congratulating her on her marriage to Philip of Spain. Anne ended her letter with the words 'from my poor house at Hever'. This was a conventional way of concluding a letter—it was not a criticism of the residence.

Later evidence suggests that Anne generally directed her interests to clothes, needlework and cooking, not politics. For instance, Marillac continued to send reports to France about her appearance and interests. He wrote in September 1541 'Madame de Cleves, who far from appearing disconsolate, is unusually joyous, and takes all the recreation she can in diversity of dress and pastime'. Her portraits show her wearing splendid and elaborately decorated dresses. We have already seen that at Cleves her major pastime seems to have been needlework—an interest which she probably kept up in England. For example, the inventory of her house at Bletchingley includes various items of 'pullinwork' (*opus pulvinarium*)—a cross or canvas stitch covering squares which were counted by the threads of the basic fabric. Sometimes it was described as 'mosiac work' because the patterned area was covered with small square stitches, giving the effect of a tessellated pavement. Because the stitches were firmly set in place, pullinwork was strong enough to withstand friction and it was used to decorate items such as cushion covers, foot carpets and kneeling mats. For this reason, it was sometimes known as 'cushion work'. We know that Anne worked a great deal in this style and introduced German designs to this country. Attractive designs for this kind of work can be found in German pattern-books of the period, and she brought with her a taste for such Flemish and German Renaissance designs. At Bletchingley, even after she had given up the house, there were various cupboard carpets, wall hangings, window curtains and bed curtains, all of pullinwork, perhaps worked by Anne and her ladies.[5]

Her interest in cookery shows in her orders to Cawarden in January and February 1556 to stock his house at Blackfriars in London to be ready for a forthcoming visit that she was planning. She ordered a great number of items, including wine, 'Gascoyne, Malmesey, Muscadel and Sacke', spices such as ginger, cinnamon, cloves, mace and pepper, together with fresh meat and the best quality wheat flour. In addition, she asked Cawarden to supply different kinds of fish—carp, pike, tench and other fresh fish. Since the fish were to be 'privately drest in her Grace's laundress's kitchen for the tryall of cookery', Anne may have been experimenting with new recipes. The account included an order for mutton, chickens and rabbits, but the emphasis on fish suggests that she was intending to try out different ways of cooking fish during the coming Lent. Perhaps she had taken note of the recommendations of Dr Andrew Boorde, who had published the first edition of his *Dietary of Health* in 1542. He keenly recommended England for its fish—'of all nations and countries, England is best served of fish, not only of all manner of sea-fish, but also of fresh-water fish and of all manner of sorts of salt-fish'. Boorde also favoured plenty of wine in the diet since it 'quickens a man's wits, comforts the heart and cleanses the liver'. Her will contains further evidence for her interest in cookery since she made a special bequest to Michael Apsley, 'clerk of our kitchen', over and above his formal wages, 'for pains taken with us over sundry ways'.[6] As another sign of her interest in food, Cawarden's rent for the house at Bletchingley included an annual payment of 12 haunches of venison from the deer parks there.

She seems to have been troubled by ill-health from time to time. When she was forced to stay in bed for a while, rumours quickly spread that she had given birth—even on one occasion to a 'fairre boy', whose father was the King. There was no truth in these rumours but there is evidence for her poor health. In 1542 her receiver, Wymond Carew, passed a message from Anne to John Gate of the Privy Chamber. She was staying at Richmond at the time and she was upset to discover that, although she had made enquiries of Dr Butts about Henry's health, the King was not aware of her concern for him. Carew wrote 'She has since been very sad as if she thought the King did not accept (receive) her gentle sending. Get my brother Denny to declare her gentleness to the King'. At the same time Carew passed on Anne's request for some cramp rings, like those that had been sent to the Duchess of Suffolk. Anne went on to say that she was not 'best at ease'.[7] Cramp rings were gold finger rings, blessed by the King on Good Friday, which were said to cure cramps, convulsions, epileptic fits and all kinds of diseases because of the power of a royal blessing. In the early part of Mary's reign, a special service was drawn up for the consecration of cramp rings—they were placed in a dish and a blessing was recited over them. Because the information about cramp rings is so general and because they seem to have been used as universal remedies, we cannot tell why Anne was asking for them. However, among Dr Butts' prescriptions for Henry's ulcerated leg, details of one preparation for Anne of Cleves have survived. It was the kind of remedy that was intended to soothe, comfort and dull the pain brought on by cold and draughts—'A plaster for my Lady Anne of Cleves, to mollify, resolve, comfort and cease pain of cold and windy causes'. The ingredients, which included linseed, camomile and hyssop suggest that she was suffering from muscular pains and inflammation.

We know that when Anne was at Richmond in March 1542, she was ill with a tertian fever—a recurrent fever that subsided for a day and then returned.[8] While acknowledging the skills of Dr Butts, Dr Boorde had published a *Breviary of Health* in which he quoted a remedy for the tertian fever. He recommended keeping the sufferer in bed, putting on plenty of bed-coverings to bring on a sweat for three or four hours and administering liquid refreshment through goose quills. Boorde suggested that, in the next stage of treatment, the patient should have plenty of ale and 'posset ale'. Posset ale was a mixture of hot milk and cold ale and was the standard remedy for 'hot fevers'. According to Boorde, this course of treatment should be repeated three times and was very successful. He boasted about his cures—'I have made many hundreds whole'.[9] On the occasion of Anne's illness, the King made enquiries about her health and put his doctors at her disposal. She also had her own doctors and attendants. We have seen that Dr Cepher died at Bletchingley—he was 'doctor of physick to my lady's Grace'—and in her will she mentioned special bequests to his replacement, Dr John Symonds, to Alarde, her surgeon and servant, and to her nurse, Mother Lovell, 'for her attendance upon us in this time of our sickness'.

XVI   Political Intrigue

While Anne seems to have been genuinely content to live with a fairly small household in quiet domesticity, others were ready to turn her situation to their political advantage. And, in spite of Henry's obvious passion for Catherine, there was often an undercurrent of rumours about his relationship with Anne. For example, as early as May 1541, Chapuys, the Spanish ambassador, was reporting the latest court gossip, saying that when Henry asked Catherine why she was looking so sad and thoughtful one day, the Queen said it was due to a rumour that he would take back Anne of Cleves as his wife. In Chapuys' version of events, Henry replied that she was wrong to believe such rumours and, even if he had to marry again, he would never choose Anne of Cleves. The ambassador supported this view, considering that it was Henry's custom never to feel affection for anyone he had once loved and then abandoned. In Chapuys' opinion, only exceptional political pressures on the continent would drive Henry once more into a union with Anne of Cleves.

During the second half of 1541 Henry and Queen Catherine spent four months on a spectacular journey to York and back to London. Tents and pavilions, displays and pageants formed the magnificent backdrop to the royal progress. It was on the scale of the Field of Cloth of Gold in its dazzling display. There were thousands of horses on the move. Silver and gold plate and colourful tapestries were brought from London to impress the population with the splendour of the court. The streets where the procession passed were gaily decorated and receptions were held for the royal visitors at stopping places along the way. It was a brilliant progress. The journey was enlivened with hunting expeditions and entertainments, but its prime purpose was to demonstrate Henry's political power. This was Henry's answer to the Pilgrimage of Grace—the rebellion of the midland and northern counties that had brought his reign into a state of crisis in 1536.

However the brilliance of the triumphant royal progress was quickly dimmed. On the return to London, Henry's love for Catherine suffered a severe setback when Thomas Cranmer, Archbishop of Canterbury, supplied him with information about her love affairs—some of these were alleged to have occurred before her marriage to Henry and some afterwards. Thomas Culpeper, a gentleman of the King's Privy Chamber, was named as her secret lover, who had visited her by the back stairs while she and the King were on their royal journey to York. Under torture, Culpeper admitted to many private meetings with Catherine, but he consistently denied that they had ever committed adultery. Henry was very unwilling to believe the evidence against his beloved Catherine, but he was finally convinced and she was executed in February 1542.

The sudden and dramatic downfall of Catherine focused attention once more on Anne of Cleves. As early as November 1541, when Cranmer was beginning to produce the evidence against Catherine, Chapuys was reporting the gossip. He wrote to the Queen of Hungary telling her about Catherine and saying that he suspected that Convocation would shortly be summoned to cancel the nullity declaration of the Cleves marriage. He also wrote to Charles V, saying 'it is said that the Lady of Cleves greatly rejoiced at the event and is coming to, if not already at, Richmond, to be near the King'. However, the ambassador was doubtful about a remarriage, saying that Henry had not gone to visit Anne, as people were expecting. He also voiced his doubts about her suitability as Queen of England, referring to her age, her fondness for wine and her 'indulging in other excesses'. In fact, he seemed to consider that Henry had been completely justified in divorcing her.[1]

Marillac took a rather different view when he reported the same news to Francis I. He was more inclined to favour the idea of a remarriage:

> As to whom the King will take, everyone thinks it will be the lady he has left, who has conducted herself very wisely in her affliction and is more beautiful than she was and more regretted and commiserated than Queen Catherine (of Aragon) was in like case.

All this was just current court gossip in November, but by December there was the further news that Anne had given birth to a son and Henry was rumoured to be the father. Chapuys again reported that, in spite of deliberate stories being spread to show that there was no connection between Anne and Henry, she had, in fact, gone away from London because she was pregnant and the child had been born in the previous summer. Henry's private life was the cause of some concern. The rumours and gossip about Anne's pregnancy and Catherine's adultery were circulating at the same time through the court and both matters were being formally discussed at meetings of the King's advisers. The rumour about Anne's child was first mentioned at a meeting of the King's officials on December 7th, when a thorough investigation was ordered to discover the truth about it. The officials of her household were particularly blamed for not passing on the information to the King. On December 9th, the members of the King's Privy Council announced that they had summoned Sir William Goring and Jasper Horsey, who were the chief officers of Anne's household, and Dorothy Wingfield, one of the ladies of her Privy Chamber, to appear before them as part of the investigation procedure.

As well as Anne's household coming under suspicion, the investigation spread further and members of the King's own household were also implicated in the scandal. Two of these, Richard Taverner and Mrs Frances Lilgrave, were accused of spreading slander. Since Taverner held a position in the royal household as a clerk of the signet office and members of the Lilgrave family were court embroiderers, they were well-placed to pick up and spread court gossip. Jane Rattsey, a member of Anne's household, admitted that she knew about the gossip but she stubbornly refused to disclose any more information. As a result, she was kept in the custody of the Lord Chancellor.

According to Chapuys, these people were imprisoned for saying that Catherine's behaviour was a judgement from God and that Anne of Cleves was Henry's true wife. It is evident that Lilgrave was imprisoned on the grounds that she had openly slandered Anne of Cleves and, by doing so, had also slandered the King. She claimed, in her defence, that she was only repeating what she had heard, but she refused to name the originator of the slander. Taverner was sent to the Tower, both for concealing Lilgrave's action and for continuing to repeat the slander himself.

When she heard about the disgrace of Catherine Howard, Rattsey was alleged to have said to Elizabeth Bassett—'What if god worketh this work to make lady Anne of Cleves Queen again?' But Rattsey's defence was that she had spoken these words as an idle remark when Bassett was praising the Lady Anne and criticizing Queen Catherine. When Rattsey was asked why she said 'What a man is the King! How many wives will he have?' She stated that she had used these words in surprise when she heard the news about Catherine's downfall. Rattsey was also questioned about Anne's alleged pregnancy and the birth of a boy who had supposedly been conceived at Hampton Court. Since uttering slander against the King and asserting the validity of the Cleves' marriage was a treasonable offence, the members of the Privy Council went to great lengths to track down this particular piece of slander. Eventually, the story came out that Taverner had heard of it from his mother-in-law and his wife, who had in turn heard it from Lilgrave and 'the old Lady Carew'. Taverner kept the news secret for a while and then told Dr Cox, who was tutor to the young Prince Edward. Cox reacted by passing on the information to the Lord Privy Seal.

The rumours were totally unfounded but the investigations suggest that the story originated with members of the Carew family, who may have had a grudge against Anne. Certainly, Wymond Carew and his wife felt aggrieved and had lodged a complaint because they received lower wages and less respect than Anne's steward, Jasper Horsey, and his wife. In addition, Anne was displeased with Carew when she discovered that he had been placed in her household for the purpose of spying on her and passing on information about her and her activities—perhaps he had been over-zealous in his reports, which had then been exaggerated by others.[2] Apart from Carew, the other members of her household seemed to have remained constantly loyal in their support for Anne.

As soon as the rumours had subsided, the Duke of Cleves strenuously began campaigning for Anne to be restored as Queen of England to replace Catherine. He took action almost immediately and in November 1541 Chapuys was speculating about special meetings of Parliament and Convocation to cancel the original divorce. Already by December the ambassadors from Cleves were bringing letters from Olisleger, promoting the cause of Anne of Cleves. Cranmer wrote to the King saying that he had received letters from Olisleger which included generalities about Anne but, when Cranmer made further enquiries and questioned the ambassadors more closely, he found that Olisleger's true aim was reconciliation and remarriage. This left Cranmer with a dilemma; he was uncertain about how to proceed, but seeing what had happened to Cromwell when he tried to promote the marriage in the first place, Cranmer was understandably reluctant to support ideas of remarriage and nothing came of the plan. While rumours about Anne and her prospects of remarriage were being generally circulated, the King and his advisers were examining a printed tract produced in France, supposedly in the name of Anne of Cleves, attacking Henry for divorcing her. Anne's cause clearly attracted more interest abroad than in England—no powerful English faction or family saw any political advantage in supporting an ex-queen.[3]

In March 1542 her illness aroused Henry's concern but there was no mention of remarriage and Anne apparently concentrated on her personal interests.

In January 1543 the Spanish ambassador was hinting at secret dealings between Cleves and England and, at the same time, he managed to suggest that the other ambassadors at the English court looked upon the envoy from Cleves as a figure of fun because of his modest way of life. He referred disparagingly to 'the ambassador, or agent, of Cleves (for though he calls himself an ambassador, he lodges in a tavern and has only one servant'). However, the man may have been genuinely acting on behalf of the Duke of Cleves, since he had been at court three or four times during the previous month, where he had not been seen for about two years. He had also been specially summoned there at Christmas for discussions. Perhaps Chapuys saw him as a threat to the influence of the Spanish Emperor and he tried hard to get rid of the envoy from Cleves on the orders of Charles V. But the members of the Privy Council refused to take notice of Chapuys' objections and insisted that the man was not an ambassador, but truly a representative of Anne of Cleves.[4]

Although Anne was not at court that Christmas, she spent several days there from time to time. In March 1543 the members of the King's Privy Council sent a message to her receiver, Carew, saying that Henry would be at Hampton Court and would like to have the company of the Lady Anne.[5] The King also gave her permission to visit Princess Mary whenever she wished. The two women were about the same age—Anne was just a year older than Mary—and they established a bond of friendship between them. They wrote letters to one another and remained on very friendly terms. Princess Mary's privy purse accounts include occasional sums of money paid to some of Anne's servants. One payment to a servant who brought Spanish silk for Princess Mary suggests that the two women shared an interest in clothes or needlework. Another payment recorded at Richmond in June 1543, reveals that the Princess was visiting Anne there and she seems to have made a contribution to the costs of her visit. There was money allowed from the royal accounts towards the costs of the kitchen, pantry, buttery and cellar, as well as a payment to the porters at the gate. On this occasion, Mary was travelling from Beddington, where she had been staying at the house of the late Sir Nicholas Carew who had been executed in 1539.[6] The King had taken over Carew's house and made the surrounding park part of his Surrey estates, which then extended right across the county to include Hampton Court, Nonsuch and Oatlands.

In July 1543 Henry married his sixth wife—this time his new Queen of England was the twice-widowed Catherine Parr. Chapuys suggested that Anne was bitterly disappointed when Henry married Catherine. In his opinion, she felt she had been humiliated by his marriage to a lady, 'who is by no means as handsome as she is, besides which there is no hope of her having children'. Chapuys went on to state that Anne wished to return to Germany and live with her mother. He had heard that she would like to be 'in her shirt (so to speak) with her mother, having taken grief and despair at the King's espousal of his last wife, who is not nearly so beautiful as she'. Anne's own reactions are unknown—it is true that Catherine was three years older than her and had no children by her first two husbands; however, she was a cultured, devout and highly educated woman, who made an excellent stepmother to Henry's children and comforted him in the years of his illness.

But even after Henry had married Catherine, rumours about Anne were still circulating abroad. People on the continent found it difficult to understand why the King had put her aside. Even as late as 1546, Henry's envoy at Dordrecht was being asked whether it was true that she had remarried the King and had two children by him. His reply was 'she goes and comes to court at her pleasure and has an honest dowry to live on'. Certainly, she was given a generous settlement; she was part of the royal household and she attended receptions at court in company with the Princesses Mary and Elizabeth. For example, when a large reception was organized in 1546 to greet the French ambassador, the Admiral of France, first in London and then at Hampton Court, Anne's name was written after the names of the two Princesses.[7] There seemed to be no sense of rejection or alienation at court, she was accepted as one of the royal ladies and she successfully adapted to this role.

Henry's health was deteriorating and by 1546 his ulcerated leg was so very painful that he was using a special chair or 'tram' with shafts so that he could be carried about, as if he were travelling in a kind of sedan chair. At the beginning of January 1547 there were rumours being spread that he was already dead—only a few of his advisers and his personal attendants were allowed to see him. The other members of the royal family were kept away and then, on January 28th, he died.

All the time that Henry was alive Anne was truly treated like the King's sister. She was welcome at court and the two of them corresponded amicably and exchanged presents. In spite of the ambassador's comments, it was very unlikely that she wanted to return to Cleves, where the political and religious situation had drastically changed. Her brother had been unsuccessful in his claims to Gelderland, which had been taken by force by Charles V. In addition, William had formed a marriage alliance with a member of the Spanish Emperor's family and any prospect of reforms in the Catholic church in Cleves had vanished.

Anne's brother, Duke William, had also encountered numerous problems. These arose from his former expansionist policies in the lower Rhine, where his power base had given him the opportunity to be at the centre of the opposition to the imperial ambitions of Charles V. As part of this policy, he had formed an alliance with Francis I and, at Francis' instigation, he married the French royal lady, Princess Jeanne of Navarre. However, Charles saw William's actions as a threat to his own powers and, in the summer of 1543, he finally moved against Duke William. He launched a military attack against him and, when the French failed to come to his aid, William was forced to make peace. By the treaty of Venlo, William lost control of Gelderland and gave up all his alliances with the enemies of the Emperor. He retained Julich and the other duchies, but his French marriage was declared invalid and, to cement the alliance between Cleves and the empire, he married Maria, the third daughter of Ferdinand, brother of Charles V. Finally, he had to accept traditional Catholic beliefs in Cleves once more and abandon all his political ambitions.

Anne's elder sister, Sibylla, also suffered because of political upheavals. While, unlike Anne, her marriage remained intact, her husband John, Duke of Saxony, was defeated and imprisoned by Charles V.

Viewed against this background, Anne's fate seems relatively fortunate. During Henry's lifetime she was well treated—she was one of the group of royal ladies and was often seen at court. However, the accession of Edward VI at the age of nine brought changes to her life; she was no longer the King's sister, but an embarrassing reminder of earlier times. Although the divorce settlement had stated that she was free to marry, all the time that Henry was alive, her status was still clouded with uncertainty. Perhaps if she had returned to Cleves, she might have married again, but remarriage in England would probably have caused her to lose much of her income there. Also, it would have been a bold and perhaps unwise political move for any man to seek to marry Henry's ex-queen during the King's lifetime. After Henry died, she could now be legitimately regarded as a widow. At the age of 31, she was a woman of no political importance, who was free to marry anyone she wished, but she chose to remain single. There were always rumours in circulation that she wished to return to Cleves, but nothing came of them. Although she was rarely at court after Henry died, a constant feature in her life was the friendship of the two Princesses, Mary and Elizabeth. Anne also drew comfort from the presence of Conrad Heresbach, the associate of Erasmus and former tutor to her brother William. Heresbach came to England as an envoy of the Duke and was warmly welcomed by Anne. However, religious and financial difficulties preoccupied her—the Protestants were in the ascendant in England and inflation was rampant.

As another sign of change, the new treasons that had been brought in during the reign of Henry VIII were now abolished. Several of these related to the King's various marriages. For example, during his lifetime it had been treasonable to declare that his marriage to Anne of Cleves had any validity. This was the reason that the gossip and various rumours about her remarriage to him were taken so seriously, since spreading them had been a treasonable offence. But at the beginning of the reign of Edward VI, such slander against Anne of Cleves was no longer of any importance. The new King of England was a boy of considerable intellectual ability. His own diary, or *Chronicle*, which he kept for about two and a half years until he died at the age of 15, reveals the extent of his powers and the diversity of his interests. His tutor, Dr Cox, was responsible for his education and the young Prince proved to be a willing pupil, since he was very quick to learn languages, music and the kind of sports that were not likely to cause him physical danger. Although he was so young, Edward had also acquired outstanding and polished skills of self-expression. We can see from his diary that, in his personal views, he followed his father's tendencies in religion—he was inclined to support reform in the existing church rather than outright Protestantism. However, because of his youth, he was kept under the guidance of powerful and influential men. These were first his uncle, the Lord Protector, Edward Seymour, who had been created Duke of Somerset, and after Somerset's downfall, John Dudley, Duke of Northumberland. Through Northumberland's influence in particular, the move towards Protestantism throughout the country was accelerated during Edward's reign.

A contemporary account relates how Protestant ideas spread into various aspects of every day life:

> Shortly after the coronation, the King, by the advice of his uncle, the Lord Protector, and others of his privy council, minding first of all to seek God's honour and glory, and thereupon intending reformation, did not only set forth by certain commissions sundry injunctions for the removing of images out of all churches, but also caused certain homilies or sermons to be drawn by sundry godly and learned men, that the same might be read in churches to the people.[1]

This pressure from the centre of the court affected Anne. Her principles of remaining a Catholic supporting reform, but not Protestantism, isolated her further from the royal household.

She was also short of money. In the later years of Henry VIII the country had suffered economic problems that continued and grew worse in Edward's reign. From about 1544 until 1551 agricultural prices had risen dramatically and they remained at this level until about 1558. Viewed against present-day price rises, the inflation of the sixteenth-century was comparatively mild but it made a great impact because it followed about 100 years of stability, when everyone had grown used to steady prices. While there had been some gradual changes in prices over the previous centuries, the dramatic suddenness of inflation took people by surprise. Different opinions were presented to explain the sudden changes. Some suggested that because sheep production was more profitable than corn, landowners had replaced corn with sheep, causing food shortages and rising prices. Others linked inflation with the debasement of the coinage in the 1540s, which made people distrustful of holding wealth in the form of coins. With hindsight, some have suggested that an influx of gold and silver from exploitation of resources in the new world led to an overall fall in the value of bullion. Such a fall in the value of money, accompanied by large increases in population numbers, could have resulted in food shortages and high prices. Certainly, high taxation and the level of government expenditure also made further demands on the coinage. In addition, the combination of coin shortages and the heavy costs of Henry's wars with France and Scotland in 1542-6 were factors that lay behind the policy of debasement. Whatever the reason may have been, debasement resulted in almost doubling the number of coins in circulation.[2]

All this had a direct effect on Anne as money values fell and Henry's original grant of £4000 had lost much of its value. We have seen that Princess Mary made certain payments towards the costs of her visit to Anne at Richmond—this may be an indication of Anne's money problems and of Mary's wish to help her. Certainly, during the last ten years of her life she was decidedly energetic and single-minded in the pursuit of an income which she felt was her due. Because of her changed circumstances, her household officials, led by her new chamberlain, Sir John Guildford, made a plea to the King's officials for an additional £126 to make up the difference. They agreed to pay the money and also arranged to add £180 for the maintenance of her household, to be paid annually until the King reached the age of 18. She was forced on several occasions to make similar pleas; her requests were never turned down, but they are evidence of her shortage of money. She apparently saw no reason to scale down her expenses or reduce the size of her household. However, in spite of making loud protests about her money difficulties, she was able to send presents to her brother in Cleves.

At the same time as Anne made her first request for money, pressure was put on her to give up her title to the house at Bletchingley. Cawarden, who had been honoured by Henry with a knighthood in 1544, still held the post of her steward there; he was very fond of the house and was keen for her to give up possession so that he could have it for himself. We have already seen how he complained about her neglect of the buildings and about the way in which her staff took valuable timber trees from the park for firewood. Cawarden was in a strong position; he was a close friend of the young King, he was a member of the King's Privy Chamber, he was keeper of Nonsuch, where Edward spent the early years of his reign, and master of tents and revels. In his capacity as master of revels, he gave much pleasure to the young Prince with his displays, pageants and entertainments. His reforming views on religion also placed him in the forefront of the Protestant revolution of Edward's reign.

In this situation, it was not difficult for Cawarden to use his influence to gain possession of this considerable country house with its many acres of parkland. To encourage Anne to give up Bletchingley, she was offered Penshurst Place in Kent as compensation. At the time, Penshurst was held by the King and was readily available to be made over to her. The King's advisers stressed the advantages of Penshurst to her, pointing out that, similar to Bletchingley, it had considerable deer parks and was near to Hever Castle, which was also in Kent, where she stayed from time to time. Penshurst Place, which has been described as 'one of Kent's oldest and greatest houses', has a long history of adaptation to new uses.[3] Like Bletchingley, it had fomerly belonged to the third Duke of Buckingham. In 1519 the Duke entertained Henry VIII at Penshurst in very lavish style. Following the Duke's execution in 1521, the King took over this house with its medieval great hall, extensive private apartments and many lodgings for servants. Work had been carried out on the house in the early sixteenth century, either by the Duke or the King. At this date some of the upper levels were added and they formed part of a three-storied range of buildings. It was certainly an attractive house in a beautiful setting but, being more than 30 miles from London, it made Anne more remote than ever from the court and royal circles. Perhaps because of its distance from London, she did not spend much time there, although, as with Bletchingley, she continued to stay at the house even after it had passed to others. For example, Sir Ralph Fane was responsible for repairs in 1550 and two years later Edward VI granted the house to Sir William Sidney.

As an extra inducement to withdraw from Bletchingley, she was offered the house at Dartford in Kent, which Henry had built in the 1540s. The King had taken over the Dominican priory there at the time of the dissolution, and Anne had stayed at the priory when she first arrived in England. However, Henry had demolished most of the ecclesiastical buildings and replaced them with a royal residence which would provide him with comfortable accommodation when he travelled between London and the Kent coast. With its 40 rooms, it was smaller than Bletchingley, but followed the same pattern, having the same kind of double-courtyard layout. While Anne accepted the exchange, perhaps reluctantly, she did not give up Bletchingley entirely; she still leased it to Cawarden and stayed there on occasions. Cawarden quickly took advantage of the exchange, which also granted him the patronage of the parish church of Bletchingley. He immediately stripped the church of most of its ornaments, particularly the items of gold and silver plate, and had them transferred to his London home at Blackfriars.[4] At about the same time that he acquired the main house at Bletchingley he seems to have demolished the house known as Hextalls, which had served him as the keeper's house within the deer park. Presumably, there was no longer any need for two such large houses so close together.

In addition, Anne was urged to give up Richmond Palace for the use of the King. As at Bletchingley, she seems to have spent hardly any money on repairs and maintenance and, soon after Edward came to the throne, the surveyor of the King's works had a warrant for £1000 to cover the costs of new building work there. Then again, in the following year, there was another grant of just over £1000 for Richmond. From the state of both these houses, we can guess that Anne lived up to the limit of her income and was unwilling to set aside money for repairs. Perhaps she felt such upkeep should be the King's responsibility, not hers.[5]

There are other definite signs of her money problems. The Duke of Somerset had been appointed by Henry VIII as protector of the young King Edward until he should reach the age of 18. It was to Somerset that Anne made her first direct appeals for money. In May 1548 she came to court to complain to the Duke about her lack of money and, in particular, about her need for adequate recompense for giving up Richmond to the King. She must also have contacted her brother for help since he sent his envoys to Edward, to ask him to ensure that Anne received payment of arrears which were due to her, to enable her to pay the wages for her household. Again in 1551, other envoys from Cleves were in England, accompanied this time by Olisleger, the son of the Duke's chancellor, with the request that the King should provide an adequate income for her. Fortunately Cranmer remained sympathetic to her and pleaded for money on her behalf. As a result, an agreement was made to pay her bills.[6] After Somerset was executed in January 1552 for plotting against other members of the Privy Council, there is further evidence for the financial difficulties that she was having to face. Anne wrote to her brother in despair 'God knows what will happen next; and everything is so costly here in this country that I do not know how I can run my house'.[7]

In 1552 she was writing from Bletchingley to Princess Mary, begging for her help in carrying through some further exchanges of property. Because the King wanted to take over her property that had formerly been part of Bisham Abbey in Berkshire, she was offered Westhorpe Hall in Suffolk instead, which she reluctantly accepted. This was the large country house built by Charles Brandon, Duke of Suffolk, between 1515 and 1530. She already had large amounts of property in Suffolk; much of it had once belonged to the Duke. But the negotiations for the exchange had taken nearly a year and she had suffered considerable loss of income from the rents during that time. Princess Mary was also involved in making exchanges of her own property at the same time and Anne hoped to speed up the procedures by enlisting her help.

When the young King died in July 1553 after a reign of just seven years, Lady Jane Grey briefly held the throne as the focus of Protestant political power, until she was deposed and executed. She was succeeded by Edward's elder sister, Mary. This was a situation that Henry had desperately tried to avoid. He was very fearful of the consequences of having a woman on the throne since he felt the security of the country would be under threat. His anxiety to produce a male heir had dominated so much of his reign because he feared the instability of a woman's rule. But now there was no alternative. Since Mary was a staunch Catholic, there was an immediate change and the old form of religion was restored.

This was probably welcome to Anne of Cleves, who retained her friendly relationship with Mary and was always well-received by her. On the day before Mary's coronation in September 1553, Anne travelled in the coronation procession in the same coach as Princess Elizabeth. The two women rode together 'in a chariot having a covering of cloth of silver, all white, and six horses trapped the like'. At the coronation dinner that followed in Westminster Hall, Princess Elizabeth and Anne of Cleves both sat at the Queen's table. However, the Spanish ambassador writing to Charles V noted that, when mass was sung, not once a day, but six or seven times a day, neither Princess Elizabeth nor Anne of Cleves was present.

We have seen that Anne generally kept out of politics, but there was just one occasion when she seemed to have taken up a particular cause. Over the years there had been many plans to find a husband for Mary—including one to marry her to Anne's brother, William. However, after Mary's coronation, when new marriage plans were again circulating, Anne suggested to her that she should marry Ferdinand, Archduke of Austria and brother of the Emperor, Charles V. It is impossible to know Anne's motives in this action; she may have thought she was helping her brother by using her influence on his behalf, since he too had now married into the Spanish royal family. However, Anne's suggestion was not followed up and Mary married Philip of Spain, son of Charles V. At the time of the wedding, Anne wrote her a letter of congratulations, wishing her 'joy and felicity'.

Queen Mary's coronation was Anne's last public appearance; from then on she led a very private existence. The Spanish ambassador, writing to Charles V, hinted that she was planning to return to Cleves. In his opinion, she was trying to use her friendship with Mary to get her marriage declared legitimate so that she would have the status of Queen Dowager. This would allow her to claim her dowry and take it with her when she left England. By trying to make her position formally legitimate, Anne may have been preparing a way of returning to Cleves more acceptably as a widow, rather than as a rejected wife. In the event, nothing came of such a plan and Anne remained in England, concentrating her energies on her domestic interests.

While Anne had not supported the growth of Protestantism in the reign of Edward VI, some of her staff were sympathetic to Protestant ideas. This had been acceptable in Edward's time, but caused trouble under Mary's Catholic regime. In addition to the financial worries that she had suffered in Edward's reign, Anne was now faced with religious threats against certain members of her household. Cawarden continued as her steward, but his strongly held Protestant views meant that he was always under suspicion and in May 1554 the Privy Council appointed Sir George Throckmorton to take charge of Anne's household, referring to him as a person 'whom the Lady is desirous to have'. Certainly, Anne was granted the freedom to choose whom she wanted to serve her in her household, but several of her servants seem to have become unacceptable to the new regime.

In September 1556 a commission, headed by the Lord Chancellor and the Lord Treasurer, summoned four of Anne's servants to appear before them at the Archbishop of Canterbury's palace in Croydon. They named the servants as Jasper Brockehouse, Otho Wyllik, Stephen Vaughan and Thomas Chare. Because of their troublesome attitude and probably because of their religious views, Brockehouse and his wife and Wyllik were ordered to leave Anne's household immediately and never enter her property again, nor have any part in her administration. The order stated 'they should come never after in any of the Lady's houses or meddle in the administration of the management of her household as her servant or officer'. Since Brockehouse and Wyllik had both come originally from Cleves they were given a few weeks' grace to leave England and they were ordered not to return, or if they did, it would be 'at their utmost peril'. Boorde, in his contemporary description of nationalities, particularly noticed the truculence of people from Gelderland and Cleves. He quoted a typical inhabitant of Gelderland who had been brought up in Cleves—a man who loved brawling and war and fighting night and day, always poor and hungry, and never changed his style of dress. Although Boorde clearly presented a caricature of the man, his description emphasized the man's troublesome nature. Perhaps Brockehouse and Wyllik were men of similar temperament. There is no evidence for the fate of the others. Cawarden was also placed under house arrest at Blackfriars for conspiring to overthrow the Catholic Queen and replace her with Elizabeth.[8]

As always, Anne took no part in any such intrigues. In her later years she spent time at Dartford in the house that Henry had built, close to the priory where she had stayed in the days before her wedding. Only part of the gatehouse now survives. The house lacked the large deer parks of Richmond and Bletchingley, but her grant of the property included a park, while the house had an extensive layout of formal gardens. It was perhaps less imposing than her other houses, but may have been more comfortable for her. There was no great hall for the formal entertainment of courtiers and any visitors were expected to wait in the chamber at the head of the stairs. It had been deliberately built in this way, without a great hall, because of Henry's wish to move away from formal public entertaining, replacing it with more private arrangements. This may have suited Anne, with her modest income and household. She may also have been pleased with the arrangement of the privy kitchen next to her own apartments, where meals could be provided at short notice and at convenient times—the main kitchen was bound by routine and was organized to supply meals only at fixed times. Since Henry had built the house between 1541 and 1544, it was still relatively new and it had all the most up-to-date features, such as a splendid new main kitchen with three great fireplaces, a pastry house, larders and a scullery close by, all served by new drains.[9] The King had his own lodgings; the Queen's apartments there included a presence chamber, privy chamber, bed-chamber, wardrobe, chapel and a closet, together with a dining chamber and withdrawing chamber. Dartford provided Anne with a relatively small and comfortable home in her later years—it was also conveniently close to London. In addition to the house, she held other property nearby which included a park, a number of dwelling-houses and an inn, known as *The Three Cups*.[10] While staying at Dartford, she ordered Cawarden to lay in a stock of items at his house in Blackfriars for her next visit to London. We have already looked at some of the items as evidence for her interest in cookery—she ordered wine and plenty of beer (a natural drink for a Dutchman, according to Boorde), spices, flour, meat and fish—but she also specified other practical necessities such as 16 dozen earthenware pots, loads of charcoal and firewood, wax for candles, wax tapers and torches. Although she had leased the estate at Bletchingley to Cawarden, she stayed there from time to time, and she may have had similar reciprocal arrangements concerning his house at Blackfriars, so that she sometimes stayed there on her visits to London. We can see from Cawarden's accounts that she lacked the money to pay for the items she ordered him to provide and she promised to pay him at a later date. He paid for the fresh fish, as it came from his larder; he also supplied new kitchen equipment such as pewter dishes, kettles, skillets, skimmers, knives and flesh-hooks, and replaced broken pots and pans and other cooking equipment, without charge. However, since these remained permanently in the house, he retained the use of them. Cawarden's house at Blackfriars was small in comparison with the other houses that Anne used, amounting to just about a dozen rooms in total.[11] It forms a striking contrast with her first home in England—the great royal palace at Greenwich.

She generally spent her time in modest style at the head of her own court, away from public life. We have already seen that she suffered from various undefined illnesses from time to time. Eventually, her health gradually deteriorated and then she suddenly grew much worse in July 1557. At the time, she was staying at the manor-house of Chelsea, which lay in Cheyne Walk—'at the King and Queen's majesties place of Chelsea, beside London.' It would have been a pleasant house for her to stay at, with attractive gardens containing cherry trees, peach trees, roses, lavender and rosemary.[12] Knowing that death was near, she made her will on July 12th and 15th 1557. She died shortly afterwards, on July 18th, at the age of 41. Her death was announced to the Queen's advisers and Queen Mary was immediately concerned that she should be 'honourably buried according to the degree of such an estate.'[13]

Anne's confessor and chaplain, Dennis Thomas, was one of the witnesses of her will, in which she asked to be buried as a Catholic. From her will, we can identify the people for whom she had the most regard. In drawing it up, she showed very close attention to detail and a concern to reward her immediate friends and the members of her household, while at the same time, giving alms to the poor. She provided for her staff to have their wages paid, together with enough black cloth for a gown and hood each for the funeral. To Dorothy Wingfield and other ladies who were her close associates she left sums of money ranging from £10 to £100. She left £10 to her laundress, Elizabeth Eliot, whose kitchen she had used for her experiments in cookery; she left the same amount to Mrs Lovell, the nurse of her sick-room. All the children in her household received 10s each and she left to her brother, the Duke of Cleves, a ring of gold and diamonds, and to his wife, she left a ring containing 'a great rock ruby'. Anne's younger sister, the Lady Amelia, who had remained unmarried in Cleves, received a diamond ring. To the Duchess of Suffolk and the Countess of Arundel, the English noblewomen who were her particular friends, she left rings of gold and diamonds. She specified that other plate, jewels and robes should be sold to pay her debts and legacies and pay for her funeral expenses. Among these legacies, she made special bequests to her physician and her surgeon—'to Dr Symonds, our physician, towards his great pains, labours and travails, taken oft-times with us: £20; and to Alarde, our surgeon and servant: £4.' She also left money for the poor of Richmond, Bletchingley, Hever and Dartford—£4 for each parish. Such gifts imply that these were the places that she was most closely associated with. To ensure that this money would be put to most effective use, she added the practical suggestion that it should be spent by the churchwardens, on the advice of her servants who lived in those places. In addition to bequests to her English servants, she provided money for servants from Cleves to enable them to return home. She also allowed £20 to 'our late servant', Otho Wyllik, who had been banished from England by the commission at Croydon for his troublesome behaviour. Her bequest to Wyllik suggests that the banishment order issued against him was made contrary to her wishes.

She appointed four executors: Nicholas Heath, who was Archbishop of York, the Lord Chancellor, Henry, Earl of Arundel, Sir Edmund Peckham and Sir Richard Preston. To all of these she left gifts of gold, gold plate or crystal glass. Her landed property and houses reverted to the Crown.

She made Queen Mary the overseer of her will, bequeathing to her the best jewel in her collection, in the hope that Mary would ensure that the will would be faithfully executed. To Princess Elizabeth she gave her second best jewel, with the plea that the Princess should take Dorothy Curzon 'one of our poor maids', into her service. Her final request was for a Catholic funeral–'that we may have the suffrages of holy church according to the Catholic faith, wherein we end our life in this transitory world.'[14]

The Queen complied with Anne's request for a Catholic burial and provided a most magnificent funeral for her. On August 4th her hearse was taken from Chelsea to Charing Cross and, at 5 pm, a great funeral procession set off from Charing Cross to Westminster. The company of mourners was led by men-at-arms carrying 12 banners, clergymen, singers, monks and yeomen, wearing black and carrying torches. These were followed by two heralds and 30 gentlemen and 20 ladies of her household on horseback, then came two other heralds with the Bishop of London and Abbot of Westminster. Some of her ladies travelled on the carriage with the hearse, which was drawn by four horses and decorated with coats of arms. Behind the hearse came Anne's own horse, with no rider but saddled and apparelled 'after the best manner'. Then came the officers of her household, some carrying white staves. They were followed by about 20 lords and ladies, all on horseback. A pen and ink drawing of her funeral procession, now in the British Library, shows the hearse, with her ladies travelling on it, and the order of mourners. It also depicts two of her executors, Peckham and Preston, accompanied by William Howard, the Lord Admiral. The chief mourner was Elizabeth, the Marchioness of Winchester, wife of the Lord Treasurer and Lord Privy Seal to Queen Mary. The procession reached Westminster Abbey where the choir was decorated with hangings and floor-coverings of sumptuous black cloth. The hearse was left there all night, with countless wax candles burning around it. On the morning of August 5th, mass was celebrated in the presence of Lord Howard and other lords and ladies, together with members of Anne's household. The Abbot of Westminster preached a sermon on the psalms of David before the requiem mass, then 12 of her officers carried her coffin to its grave. She was buried

'Prince-like' on the right of the choir, then her officials broke their white staves and put them into the grave. Afterwards, all the nobles and officials left to take dinner, given by the Marquis of Winchester, at Anne's expense—'at her Grace's costs and charges'.

She was buried with great ceremony near the high altar in Westminster Abbey. But according to Henry Machyn's diary of London, which covers the years 1550-63, her richly-decorated hearse was soon robbed of its splendid ornaments of gold cloth, velvet, and banners. Machyn wrote 'On the 22nd of August the hearse of Anne of Cleves was taken down, by night-time the monks had removed all the velvet cloth, coats of arms and banners—such a thing had never been done before'. Machyn had a particular interest in the burial, since he was a supplier of funeral trappings and kept records of the principal funerals for which he provided equipment. Her tomb still lies in Westminster Abbey but nowadays it is difficult to see it since it is partly hidden by other monuments. On one of two panels on each side of her tomb it is just possible to decipher the initial letters A and C, surmounted by a crown. The carved decoration also shows a skull and crossbones, as symbols of mortality. The tomb was reckoned to have been carved by a craftsman from Cleves, but never finished. Ironically, in spite of her status as a 'non-wife', she was the only one of Henry's wives to be buried at Westminster.[15]

Queen Mary immediately sent her condolences to Duke William of Cleves who ordered memorial services for his sister, whom he described as 'Princess Anna, Duchess of Julich, Cleves and Berg, Queen of England', to be held in every church and monastery in Cleves.

Holinshed wrote this last tribute to her in his chronicle:

The fifteenth of July, the Lady Anne of Cleves departed this life at Chelsea and was honourably buried at Westminster the fifth of August, a lady of right commendable regard, courteous, gentle, a good housekeeper and very bountiful to her servants.[16]

Within a fortnight reports and rumours were spreading through foreign courts that she died because she had been so cruelly treated in England. Henry's rejection of her even gave rise to an imposter who presented herself at the court of John Frederick in Coburg, asking for protection and security. The Prince gave her hospitality until she was finally proved to be mad.

In 1553, Simon Renard, an envoy of Spain, summed up the marriage in his letter to the Emperor Charles V:

> It was a dangerous matter to take a share in the marriage of Princes, like Cromwell, who arranged the match between the late King Henry and the daughter of Cleves, because he believed that Germany would ever afterwards assist this country for her sake, whereas the marriage only lasted one night and ruined Cromwell.[17]

Epilogue

We have traced the story of the Cleves marriage through negotiations involving ambition, political power and religious ideology. Following two years of extended discussions, events reached a climax at Rochester on a cold New Year's Day in 1540. From that one moment of bitter disappointment, Cromwell's ambitious plans of political alliance began to disintegrate.

As a result, divorce came quickly and Anne was left to make her own way in England. After a reign of just six months, she was 'a queen unqueened'—divorced, wealthy and independent. Most importantly, she made no public show of opposition. This was wise, since the unspoken threat of execution lay before her. Her major triumph was to survive in times when many lost their heads. She not only survived divorce, but survived on her own terms. She took lessons from the fate of Catherine of Aragon and admitted straightaway that the marriage had failed. Finance seems to have been a key factor in the arrangements—a comfortable settlement allowed her to live in a style appropriate for a royal lady. Whatever her private feelings may have been, the size of her award removed any sense of public humiliation or misery. She somehow solved the problem of being a woman of high status, who had no fixed place or role in society. After all, she was in a sense outside the conventions of normal society—a divorced Queen, a foreigner, with no responsibility for royal children. But in spite of being a victim of circumstances, she did not demand sympathy as a victim, nor was she banished into oblivion. Her strong character was her greatest asset and she forged a role for herself first as a kind of adopted royal aunt and then as a widow. In spite of scandal and gossip, her life was never in danger and, by keeping her mind firmly focused on her own personal interests, she presented no political threat.

Her problems chiefly began after Henry died. From that time onwards, her main preoccupation seems to have been with maintaining her income—to ensure that she could support the kind of life she found congenial. It is very likely that she could have returned to Cleves, if she wished. The fact that she chose not to return is perhaps an indication of her contentment—she had adapted herself to life in England. She soon learned the language, she had freedom and independence and was in control of her own life. She seems to have made no effort to marry again. A second marriage would have affected her status and income and brought political difficulties both for her and her husband. She may also have privately considered that she was still truly married to Henry, in spite of the divorce. If this was so, she would be unlikely to remarry during his lifetime. After he had died, she generally withdrew from court life and adapted to a form of widowhood.

This detailed study of her life after the divorce shows her as a determined, resilient, intelligent woman, who took a realistic view of her situation and made the best of it. Her practical, unemotional attitude enabled her to live in quiet enjoyment. Unfortunately, such qualities had no appeal for Henry. The failure of the marriage can be attributed to Cromwell's ambitious plans and her inability to match Henry's high hopes for his fourth bride.

Appendix

Grants awarded to Anne of Cleves as her divorce settlement:

(a) The forfeited property of Thomas Cromwell, Earl of Essex

Essex
Manors:
  Abbess Hall
  Birchall cum Horsey
  Brokehall
  Cust Hall
  Dedham
  East Horndon
  Hockley
  Langham
  Tollesbury
Farms:
  Bohun's Hall
  Charfleet
  Canewdon
  Gorwell
  Hicks Green
  High Hall
  Langham Park
  Prentice
  Ray in Southminster
  Shalford
Advowsons (right to appoint clergy):
  Langham

Leicestershire
Manor and rectory:
  Melton

Lincolnshire
Rectory:
  Sutton

Northamptonshire
Manor and advowson:
  Edgecott

Oxfordshire
Manors and advowsons:
  Broughton
  Filkins
  Standlake

Suffolk
Manor:
  Stratford near Higham
Rectory:
  Haverhill

Surrey
Farm:
  Gatton
Rent:
  £4 a year from St Olave's church, Southwark

Sussex
Manors:
  Balneath
  Brighton
  Ditchling
  Falmer
  Langney
  Nyetimber
  Otham
  Southover
  Withdean

Farms:
  Broughton
  Frithland
  Hesemans
  Hothesrove
  Knollond
  Le Wyke
  Maresfield
  Oldland
  Ovingdean
  Pigeons
  Southland
  Wantley
Rent:
  £24 a year from the barony of Lewes, which had formerly belonged partly to the priory of Lewes and to Michelham priory.
Rectories:
  Alfriston
  Brighton
  Cuckfield
  Ditchling
  East Grinstead
  Falmer
  Fletching
  Gadberton
  Iford
  Kingston-near-Lewes
  Laughton
  Patcham
  Piddinghoe
  Rottingdean
  West Hoathly
  The chapel of Wivelsfield
Tithes:
  Allington
  Ashcombe
  Atlingworth
  Balsdean
  Barcombe
  Beddingham
  Berwick
  Bevehorne in Chailey
  Clayton
  Cuckfield
  Ditchling
  Dygons land
  Eastbourne
  Gadberton
  Greatham
  Hamsey
  Hangleton
  Hardham
  Hernyngham
  Houndean
  Hurstpierpoint
  Le Hyde in Lewes
  Kingston
  Mechyng
  Moulsecoomb
  Newtimber in Saddlescombe
  Northease
  Ovindean
  Piddinghoe
  Plumpton
  Portslade
  Powntyngs
  Pyecombe
  Rodmell
  Rottingdean
  Southover
  Southwick
  Tarring
  Telscombe
  Twineham
  Wallands
  Westmeston
  Willingdon
Tithes of wool, lambs and corn of le Wyke in Patcham
Tithes of beans in Sutton
Advowsons of vicarages of churches:
  Alfriston
  Brighton
  Cuckfield
  Ditchling
  East Grinstead
  Falmer
  Fletching
  Iford
  Kingston-near-Lewes

Laughton
Patcham
Piddinghoe
Rottingdean
West Hoathly

Yorkshire
Manor and rectory:
 Halifax

(b)   The forfeited property of Sir Nicholas Carew

Surrey
 Manor and lordship of Bletchingley, with two parks and land called Hextalls
 Borough of Bletchingley and lands in Bletchingley and Godstone

(c)   Additional grants

Berkshire
Manors:
 Bray
 Cookham
 Maidenhead
 Montague

Buckinghamshire
Manors:
 Crawstons
 Great Marlow
 Little Marlow
Rectory and advowson:
 West Wycombe

Caernarvonshire
Manor:
 Beddgelert

Clwyd
Manor:
 Mold

Devonshire
Rectory and advowson:
 Stokenham

Hampshire
Rectories and advowsons:
 Ecchinswell
 Kingsclere

Isle of Wight
Rectory and advowson:
 Shalfleet

Kent
Manors, rectories and advowsons:
 Hever
 Kemsing
 Seal

London
 Sondays wharf, Baynard's castle

Norfolk
Manors:
 Claxton
 Costessy
 Hundred of Freebridge
 Hillington
 Saxlingham
 Stockton
 West Somerton
Rectories and advowsons:
 Upton
 West Somerton

Oxfordshire
Manor:
 Isle of Crowell

Somerset
Rectory and advowson:
 Curry Rivel

Suffolk
Manors:
 Bawdsey

Boyton
Chesilford
Cretingham
Cotton Brisworth
Cotton Hempnall
Culpho
Fressingfield
Frostenden
Glavering
Glemham Magna
Great Finborough
Hundred of Hartesmere
Huntingfield
Newhawe
Occold
Saxmundham Market
Stradbroke
Stratford
Hundred of Stowe
Swannes
Tangham
Thorndon
Vyrles

Walsham
Wattisfield
Hundred of Wangford and Blything
Rectories and advowsons:
Corton
Dunwich
Playford
Yaxley
Rent of Combs Manor

Surrey
Manors and advowsons:
Ham
Petersham
Richmond
Sheen

Wiltshire
Manor:
Hurdcott
Rectory and advowson:
Helmerton

Notes

Introduction

1. Hume, *Wives of Henry VIII*, pp.331-57.
2. Pollard, *Cranmer*, p.101. Scarisbrick, *Henry VIII*, pp.368-75.
3. Williamson, *Debrett's Kings and Queens*, p.124.
4. Starkey, *Rivals in Power*, pp.99-100.
5. Strickland, 'Anne of Cleves'.
6. Weir, *Six Wives of Henry VIII*, pp.429; 566-7. Fraser, *Six Wives of Henry VIII*, p.418.
7 Weir, *Six Wives of Henry VIII*, p.388.
8. Starkey, *Henry VIII*, p.143.

Chapter I

1. *Letters and Papers Foreign and Domestic*, 12, pt. 1, p.486; pt. 2, p.27. Elton, *Reform and Renewal*, p.11.
2. Nottingham University, Middleton Collection, MiC 10.
3. *L. & P.*, 12, pt. 2, pp.318-20.
4 Hall, *Henry VIII*, 2, p.285.
5. Starkey, *Rivals in Power*, p.90
6. Miller, *Henry VIII and the English Nobility*, pp.79-80.
7. Williams, *Henry VIII and his Court*, p.72.
8. Loades, *Chronicles of Tudor Kings*, p.113.
9. Williams, *Henry VIII and his Court*, p.77.
10. *Calendar of Spanish State Papers*, 6, pt. 1, pp.4-28.
11. *L. & P.*, 12, pt. 2, pp.394-453.
12. *Cal. Sp. State Papers*, 6, pt. 1, p.62.
13. Smit and Zweers, 'Der Erweb Gelderns', *passim.*

Chapter II

1. Vaughan, *Philip the Good*, pp.290-3.
2. Davis, *The Paston Letters*, 1, pp.538-40.
3. Vaughan, *Charles the Bold*, pp.48-53; 122; 140-8.
4. Hay, *Europe in the Fourteenth and Fifteenth Centuries*, pp.190-204.

5. Pettegree, *The Early Reformation in Europe*, pp.1-3.
6. Duke, 'The Netherlands', pp.142-3. MacCulloch, 'England' pp.186-9.
7. McConica, *English Humanists*, p.175. Elton, *Reformation Europe*, pp.167-8.

Chapter III

1. Beckinsale, *Thomas Cromwell*, pp.10-12. Holinshed, *Chronicles of England*, 3, p.817. Mackie, *The Earlier Tudors*, pp.251-2. Bindoff, *The House of Commons*, pp.729-34.
2. *L. & P.*, 14, pt. 1, pp.40-1.
3. Dickens, *Thomas Cromwell*, p.161.
4. *L. & P.*, 14, pt. 1, pp.191-2.
5. Ibid., pp.428-33.
6. Ibid., pp.213-4.
7. Ibid., pp.428-33.
8. *L. & P.*, pt. 2, pp.8-9.
9. Ibid., p.34.
10. Ibid., pp.66-7; 96-7. BL. Cott. Vitel. C, XI, ff.213-9.
11. Hacker & Kuhl, 'A Portrait of Anne of Cleves'.
12. Strickland, 'Anne of Cleves', p.33.

Chapter IV

1. *Cal. Sp. State Papers*, 8, pp.604-7.
2. Starkey, *Henry VIII*, pp.145-9.
3. *Cal. Sp. State Papers*, 6, pt. 1, p.200. L. & P., 14, pt. 2, pp.96-7.
4. *L. & P.*, 14, pt. 2, p.170.
5. BL. Cott. Vitel. XI, ff.221-2. *L. & P.*, 14, pt. 2, pp.4-6; 15; 129-138; 182; 200-3; 231-2; 493; 16, p.180. Holinshed, *Chronicles of England*, 3, p.811. Byrne, *Lisle Letters*, 5, pp.679; 723.

Chapter V

1. *L. & P.*, 14, pt. 2, pp.108; 160; 231-2; 238; 246-7; 263-5. *Cal. Venetian State Papers*, 4, p.285. Holinshed, *Chronicles of England*, 3, p.813. *State Papers Henry VIII*, 8, pp.208-13.

Chapter VI

1. *L. & P.*, 3, pt. 2, p.1541. *Cal. Venetian State Papers*, 4, p.286. Thurley, *Royal Palaces*, p.56. Colvin, *History of the King's Works*, 3, pp.13; 242-6; 4, pp.59-63; 457. Howard, *Early Tudor Country House*, pp.143; 207.

2.   *L. & P.*, 14, pt. 2, p.283. Toulmin Smith, *Leland*, 4, p.42. Nicolas, *The Privy Purse Expenses of Henry VIII*, p.274.
3.   Howard, *Early Tudor Country House*, p.208. Smith, *History of Rochester*, pp.305-7.
4.   *L. & P.*, 16, p.180.
5.   *L. & P.*, 15, pp.7-8.

Chapter VII

1.   Hall, *Henry VIII*, 2, pp.295-6.
2.   Hamilton, *Wriothesley's Chronicle*, 2, pp.109-12.
3.   Smollett, *History of England*, 6, p.68.
4.   *L. & P.*, 15, pp.388-90.

Chapter VIII

1.   *L. & P.*, 15, p.10
2.   Hall, *Henry VIII*, 2, pp.296-303. Holinshed, *Chronicles of England*, 3, p.814. Colvin, *History of the King's Works*, 4, pp.104-5.
3.   *L. & P.*, 15, pp.2-10.
4.   Hatfield MSS., I, p.12. *L. & P.*,13, pt.1, pp.191; 207-8.
5.   Merriman, *Life and Letters of Thomas Cromwell*, 2, p.270.

Chapter IX

1.   *L. & P.*, 15, pp.389-91. BL. Cott. Titus, B, I, ff.418-9. Colvin, *History of the King's Works*, 4, p.102.
2.   Hall, *Henry VIII*, 2, p.303. Thurley, *Royal Palaces*, p.48. *L. & P.*, 15, p.13.
3.   Colvin, *History of the King's Works*, 4, pp.286-7.
4.   *L. & P.*, 15, p.9; pp.185; 188, 193. Starkey, *Henry VIII*, pp.14; 19.
5.   *L. & P.*, 14, pt. 2, pp.280-1.
6.   *L. & P.*, 15, p.86.
7.   Hamilton, *Wriothesley's Chronicle*, 1, p.118.
8.   Robinson, *Original Letters*, 2, p.627.

Chapter X

1.   Merriman, *Life and Letters of Thomas Cromwell*, 2, pp.238-66.
2.   Hamilton, *Wriothesley's Chronicle*, 2, pp.117-9. Holinshed, *Chronicles of England*, 3, p.816.
3.   Robinson, *Original Letters*, 2, pp.201-2.
4.   Starkey, *Henry VIII*, p.121.
5.   Brigden, *London and the Reformation*, p.326.

6.   BL. Cott., Otho, C, X, ff.235-40.
7.   BL. Cott., Titus, B, I, ff.409-10; 418-9.
8.   *L. & P.*, 15, pp.365-424. Strype, *Ecclesiastical Memorials*, 1, pt. 2, pp.459-61. Goldsmid, *Historical Tracts*, pp.14-16. *Stat. Realm*, 3, pp.781-3.
9.   *Statutes at Large*, 2, p.298.

Chapter XI

1.   *L. & P.*, 15, pp.417-89. Hatfield MSS., I, pp.12-14. BL. Cott., Otho, C, X, ff.243-4. *Henry VIII*, Act 2, Scene 2.

Chapter XII

1.   Colvin, *History of the King's Works*, 4, pt. 2, p.242.   Thurley, *Royal Palaces*, pp.326-7.
2.   *L. & P.*, 15, pp.440-1; 446.

Chapter XIII

1.   *L. & P.*, 16, pp.242; 717.
2.   *L. & P.*, 15, pp.462; 484; 490. Bindoff, *The House of Commons*, 1, p.582.
3.   Thurley, *Royal Palaces*, pp.32; 179.
4.   Colvin, *History of the King's Works*, 4, pp.228-9.

Chapter XIV

1.   *Cal. Sp. State Papers*, 6, pt. 1, pp.304-5.

Chapter XV

1.   Howard, *Early Tudor Country House*, p.68.
2.   Colvin, *History of the King's Works*, 4, pp.228-9.
3.   Hist. MSS. Comm., Report 7, pp.597-611. Howard, *Early Tudor Country House*, p.126.
4.   Leveson-Gower, 'Bletchingley Church', pp.242-51. *L. & P.*, 18, pt. 2, p.284.
5.   *L. & P.*, 16, p.4. Folger Lib. LB 351; LB 505; LB 507. Norris, *Costume and Fashion*, 3, pt. 1, p.225. Alford, *Needlework as Art*, pp.204-7; 384. *Acts of the Privy Council 1550-2*, p.292.
6.   *L. & P.*, 17, p.89. Kemp, *Loseley Manuscripts*, pp.10-12. Furnivall, *Andrew Boorde*, pp.254; 268.

7.   *L. & P.*, Addenda, 1, pt. 2, p.534.
8.   Kunz, *Rings for the Finger*, pp.343-5. BL. Sl. 1047, f.30b.
9.   Furnivall, *Andrew Boorde*, p.97.

Chapter XVI

1.   *Cal. Sp. State Papers*, 6, pt. 1, pp.328; 408-9.
2.   *L. & P.*, 16, pp.612; 628; 665; 671-3.
3.   *L. & P.*, 16, p.676. Cox, *Writings and Letters of Thomas Cranmer*, pp.109-10.
4.   *L. & P.*, 18, pt. 1, pp.30; 162.
5.   *L. & P.*, Addenda, pt. 2, pp.541-2.
6.   Madden, *Privy Purse Expenses of the Princess Mary*, pp.118; 159.
7.   *Cal. Sp. State papers*, 6, pt. 2, p.447. *L. & P.*, 21, pt. 1, p.696.

Chapter XVII

1.   Jordan, *Edward VI*, pp.1-27 *passim*. Holinshed, *Chronicles of England*, 3, p.867. *Cal. Sp. State Papers*, 10, p.282
2.   Outhwaite, *Inflation in Tudor and Early Stuart England*, pp.11-45 *passim*.
3.   Nicolson, *Kent*, pp.101-2.
4.   *Acts of the Privy Council 1547-50*, pp.81; 471-2.
5.   Colvin, *History of the King's Works*, 4, p.229.
6.   *Acts of the Privy Council 1550-2*, pp.60; 480.
7.   Jordan, *Edward VI*, p.104.
8.   *Acts of the Privy Council 1554-6*, pp.29; 351-3. Holinshed *Chronicles of England*, 4, p.6. Furnivall, *Andrew Boorde*, pp.152-3. *Cal. Sp. State Papers*, 11, pp.188; 279.
9.   Thurley, *Royal Palaces*, pp.58; 156.
10. Boreham, *Dartford's Royal Manor-House*, *passim*. Colvin, *History of the King's Works*, 4, p.71.
11. Folger Lib. LB 328.
12. Colvin, *History of the King's Works*, 4, pp.64-5.
13. *Acts of the Privy Council 1556-8*, p.128.
14. Strickland, 'Anne of Cleves', pp.93-5. Nichols, *Diary of Henry Machyn*, pp.ix; 148.
15. BL. Eg. 2642, ff.184; 200; Add. MSS. 35324, f.7.
16. Holinshed, *Chronicles of England*, 4, p.88.
17. *Cal. Sp. State Papers*, 10, pp.338-9.

Bibliography

Manuscript Sources
British Library
Add. MSS. 35324
MS Cotton Otho C X
MS Cotton Titus B I
MS Cotton Vitellius C XI
MS Egerton 2809
MS RO App. 89
MS Sloane 1047

Folger Shakespeare Library
LB 328
LB 351
LB 505
LB 507

Nottingham University Library
MS MiC. 10

Printed Sources
Calendar of State Papers, Spanish, Bergenroth, G. and others, (eds.) (8 vols., London, 1862-1904).
Calendar of State Papers, Venetian, Brown, R. and others, (eds.) (39 vols., London, 1887-1947).
Historical Manuscripts Commission, Report 7, (London, 1879).
Historical Manuscripts Commission, Series 9, Hatfield Mss., (18 vols., (London, 1885-1940).
Letters and Papers, Foreign and Domestic, of the Reign of Henry VIII. Brewer, J.S. and others, (eds.) (21 vols., London, 1862-1932).
Statutes of the Realm, Luders, A. and others, (eds.) (11 vols., London, 1810-28).
Statutes at Large, Ruffhead, O. and others, (eds.) (18 vols., London, 1780).

Secondary Sources
Alford, M.M., *Needlework as Art* (London, 1886).
Beckinsale, R., *Thomas Cromwell* (London, 1978).
Bindoff, S., *The House of Commons* (3 vols., London, 1982).

Boreham, P.W., *Dartford's Royal Manor House* (Dartford, 1991).

Byrne, M., (ed.) *The Lisle Letters* (6 vols., London and Chicago, 1981).

Cameron, E., *The European Reformation* (Oxford, 1992).

Coleman, D.C., *The Economy of England 1450-1750* (Oxford, 1977).

Colvin, H.E., *The History of the King's Works* (6 vols., London, 1963-82).

Cox, J.E., (ed.) *Miscellaneous Writings and Letters of Thomas Cranmer* (Parker Society, Cambridge, 1846).

Dasent, J. and others (eds.) *Acts of the Privy Council* (46 vols., London, 1890-1964).

Davis, N., *The Paston Letters* (2 vols., Oxford, 1971-77).

Dowling, M., *Humanism in the Age of Henry VIII* (London, 1986).

Dickens, A.G., *Thomas Cromwell and the English Reformation* (London, 1977).

Duke, A., 'The Netherlands', in Pettegree, A., (ed.) *The Early Reformation in Europe* (Cambridge, 1992), pp.142-65.

Ellis, H., (ed.) *Original Letters Illustrative of English History* (11 vols., London, 1824, 1827, 1846).

Elton, G., *Reformation Europe 1517-59* (London, 1963).

Elton, G., *The Reformation 1520-59*. The New Cambridge Modern History, 2. (14 vols., Cambridge, 1957-70).

Elton, G., *Reform and Renewal* (Cambridge, 1973).

Fraser, A., *The Six Wives of Henry VIII* (London, 1992).

Furnivall, F.J., (ed.) *Boorde's Introduction and Dietary* (Early English Text Society, London, 1870).

Goldsmid, E. and G., (eds.) *A Collection of Eighteen Rare and Curious Historical Tracts and Pamphlets* (Edinburgh, 1886).

Guy, J.A., 'The Tudor Commonwealth: Revising Thomas Cromwell'. *Historical Journal*, 23, no.3 (1980) pp.681-7.

Guy, J.A., *Tudor England* (Oxford, 1988).

Hacker, P. & Kuhl, C., 'A Portrait of Anne of Cleves' in *Burlington Magazine* (March 1992, pp.172-5).

Hall, E., *Henry VIII* (2 vols., London, 1904).

Hamilton, W.D., (ed.) *Wriothesley's Chronicle* (2 vols., Camden Society, 1875).

Hasted, E., *The History of the County of Kent* (12 vols., Canterbury, 1798).

Hay, D., *Europe in the Fourteenth and Fifteenth Centuries* (London, 2nd edn., 1989).

Holinshed, R., *Chronicles of England* (6 vols., London, 1808).

Howard, M., *The Early Tudor Country House* (London, 1987).

Hume, M., *The Wives of Henry the Eighth* (London, 1905).

Ives, E.W., *Anne Boleyn* (Oxford, 1986).

Jordan, W.K., *Edward VI: The Threshold of Power* (London, 1970).

Kempe, A.J., (ed.) *Losely Manuscripts* (London, 1835).

Kunz, G.F., *Rings for the Finger* (London, 1917).

Leveson-Gower, G., 'Bletchingley Church', *Surrey Archaeological Collections*, 5, (1871) pp.227-52.

Loades, D., *Chronicles of the Tudor Kings* (London, 1990).

MacCulloch, D., 'England' in Pettegree, A., (ed.) *The Early Reformation in Europe* (Cambridge, 1992) pp.166-87.

Mackie, J., *The Earlier Tudors 1485-1558* (Oxford, 1983).

Madden, F.W., (ed.) *The Privy Purse Expenses of the Princess Mary, December 1536 to December 1544* (London, 1831).

Mawer, A., Stenton, F.M. and Gover, J., *The Place-Names of Sussex* (2 vols., Cambridge, 1930).

McConica, J.K., *English Humanists and Reformation Politics* (Oxford, 1968).

Merriman, R., (ed.) *Life and Letters of Thomas Cromwell* (2 vols., Oxford, 1902).

Miller, H., *Henry VIII and the English Nobility* (Oxford, 1989).

Nichols, J., (ed.) *Chronicle of Calais* (Camden Society, 35. 1846).

Nichols, J., *(ed.) The Diary of Henry Machyn* (Camden Society, 37. 1848).

Nicolas, N.H., *The Privy Purse Expenses of King Henry VIII* (London, 1827).

Nicolson, N., *Kent* (London, 1988).

Norris, H., *Costume and Fashion* (4 vols., London, 1924-38).

Outhwaite, R.B., *Inflation in Tudor and Early Stuart England* (2nd edn. Cambridge, 1982).

Pettegree, A., (ed.) *The Early Reformation in Europe* (Cambridge, 1992).

Pollard, A., *Thomas Cranmer* (London, 1927).

Ramsey, P.R., (ed.) *The Price Revolution in Sixteenth-Century England* (London, 1971).

Reaney, P.H., *The Place-Names of Essex* (Cambridge, 1935).

Robinson, H., (ed.) *Original Letters Relative to the English Reformation* (2 vols., Parker Society, Cambridge, 1846).

Scarisbrick, J.J., *Henry VIII* (London, 1974).

Smit, E. and Zweers, J., 'Der Erwerb Gelderns als Begwegrunnd für die Heirat zwischen Anna von Kleve und Heinrich VIII von England' in *Land im Mittelpunkt der Machte* (Dusseldorf, 1957).

Smith, F., *History of Rochester* (London, 1928).

Smollett, T.G., *History of England* (3rd edn. London,1759).

Starkey, D., *The Reign of Henry VIII* (London, 1985).

Starkey, D., (ed.) *Rivals in Power* (London, 1990).

Starkey, D., (ed.) *Henry VIII: A European Court in England* (London, 1991).

Strickland, A., *Lives of the Queens of England* (6 vols., London, 1889).

Strype, J., *Ecclesiastical Memorials* (3 vols., Oxford, 1820-40).

Thurley, S., *Royal Palaces of Tudor England* (London, 1993).

Toulmin Smith, L., (ed.) *Leyland's Itinerary* (5 vols., London, 1909).

Vaughan, R., *Philip the Good* (London, 1970).

Vaughan, R., *Charles the Bold* (London, 1973).

Warnicke, R.M., *The Rise and Fall of Anne Boleyn* (Cambridge, 1989).

Weir, A., *The Six Wives of Henry VIII* (London, 1991).

Williams, N., *Henry VIII and his Court* (London, 1971).

Williamson, D., *Debrett's Kings and Queens of Britain* (Exeter, 1986).

Wood, M., (ed.) *Letters of Royal and Illustrious Ladies* (3 vols., London, 1846).

Index

Udall, Nicholas, 86

Vendôme, Marie of, 12
Venlo, treaty of, 101

Westhorpe Hall, Suffolk, 107
Westminster Abbey, chapter house, 68; funeral of Anne of Cleves, 113-4; tomb, 114
Whitehall Palace, Westminster, 58
Wingfield, Sir Anthony, 51
Wingfield, Dorothy, 96, 112
Wingfield, Sir Richard, 9

Wolsey, Thomas, Cardinal, 9, 22-3, 58, 74
Wootton, Nicholas, English envoy in Cleves, 25-6, 33
Wyllik, Otho, 109, 112
Wriothesley, Charles, *Chronicles of England*, 46-7, 60
Wriothesley, Sir Thomas, 67

York House, Westminster, 58

Zuyder Zee, 20, 30